BOLD, PUNCHY FLAVORS, BRIGHT COLORS, AND MEALS FOR ANY DAY OF THE WEEK.

Devin Connell, chef and creator of This Is Crumb, knows that real people with busy lives want simple, delicious meals that are easy to prepare and impossible to resist. But she also knows that planning Thursday's dinner on Monday morning doesn't make a whole lot of sense. Because what happens when you see a picture of a roast chicken thigh on Instagram, and now you just *need* roast chicken? When it comes to her own kitchen, Devin wants to be free of a plan and cook what she craves. But if the thought of this non-plan plan has you breaking out in a sweat, take a deep breath and dive in to *Conveniently Delicious.* You'll soon learn that spontaneity is possible, whether you're cooking for yourself, for your partner, or for a casual gathering with friends. If you've got a kitchen that is stocked with the right basics, a combination of fresh produce and shelf-stable items, the opportunities for mixing and matching are endless.

Think of easy nibbles such as Labneh with Bursted Tomatoes & Dill; gorgeous salads like Nectarine, Baby Gem, Fried Almond & Feta; hearty vegetables such as Roasted Acorn Squash with Hazelnut & Fried Rosemary; and effortlessly impressive mains, like 10-Minute Pasta with Italian Tuna, Olives & Lemon or Salt & Pepper Flank Steak with Quick Tomato Shallot Kimchi. And, obviously, always dessert—an Upside Down Skillet Apple Crumble or a Lemon Pudding with Salted Graham Crumb is the perfect way to end a meal.

Written with Devin's sharp humor and str̶̶̶̶̶̶̶̶̶̶̶̶̶̶ absolutely stunning, sumptuous photography, *Conve̶̶̶̶̶̶̶̶̶̶̶̶̶̶̶̶̶̶̶̶̶̶* of recipes that you'll come back to again and again. As t̶̶̶̶̶̶̶̶̶̶̶, this cookbook is guaranteed to make you feel lighter about mealtimes than when you started, even if, most of the time, she's talking about how to make you feel full.

HOW TO COOK AND EAT WITH SPONTANEITY AND JOY

DEVIN CONNELL

CONVENIENTLY

DELICIOUS

appetite

by RANDOM HOUSE

Appetite by Random House™ and colophon are registered trademarks of Penguin Random House LLC.

Library and Archives of Canada Cataloguing in Publication is available upon request.

ISBN: 9780525610731
eBook ISBN: 9780525610748

Cover and book design by Kelly Hill
Photography by Louisa Nicolaou

Printed and bound in China
Published in Canada by Appetite by Random House™
a division of Penguin Random House LLC.

www.penguinrandomhouse.ca

10 9 8 7 6 5 4 3 2 1

appetite
by RANDOM HOUSE

Penguin
Random House
Canada

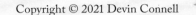

To my parents, who brought me up with
joy and love. You pushed me to fulfill
my dreams, while catching me if I fell.

To Darcy, my love and my friend for 27 years.
I don't understand life without you in it.

And to my two boys—without question the
greatest cakes I ever baked.

NIBBLES

VEGETABLES

CONTENTS

SALADS & SOUPS

WEEKEND ADVENTURES

PASTA, GRAINS & FLATBREAD

FISH

MEAT

DESSERTS

INTRODUCTION

From as far back as I can remember, my favorite moments have always centered on food: Cooking with my Belgian grandmother, baking bread with my dad or skipping summer camp to start a cookie business (just like any normal, well-adjusted teenager, right?). Growing up, family meals were a time to talk, to laugh and, of course, to eat well. I never considered the possibility that the focus of my life would be anything other than food. As they say, when you know, you know.

That single-minded focus came to fruition when, in my late 20s, I opened the first of my three cafés and bakeries, Delica Kitchen, in Toronto. I also fulfilled a lifelong dream of publishing a cookbook with my mom—an ode to our love of family, friends and the kitchen table. After several years in the restaurant business (and raising two small boys), I began to realize that there was so much more that I wanted to communicate about food and gathering. The way I ate in my early 20s was different from the way I now eat with my growing family. In my 20s, I used to relish eating alone because I could cook whatever my heart desired, whereas now, my cooking considers everyone at the table and what they might like. Feeding my family and friends, and having a kitchen bursting at the seams with mess, fun and one or two food fights, makes me happy—even though the cleanup can be much more work. For a long time, I have wanted to share all the wonderful things I've learned—whether they came from my own kitchen, my restaurants or my travels across the globe in search of new inspiration. My website, Crumb, was born as a place for all of these good bits to live.

Crumb is a lifestyle platform that celebrates the power of food to bring people pleasure, and to bring them together. To break free from meal planning. To cook—and eat—with spontaneity and joy. Crumb shares expert insights, practical tips and tools, and straightforward recipes to make easy, wholesome family meals a reality. Crumb is dedicated to celebrating life's simple pleasures: food, travel, family and entertaining, and to keeping good company along the way.

If you find yourself reading this book, I think it's safe to assume that you, like me, LOVE not just eating but being in the kitchen and cooking too. Of course, it's about getting from A to B with as little fuss as possible, but there's so much fun to be had in between, right? For those of us who love to cook, we can often get bogged down by technique (fricassee vs. concasse?!), timing (because, yeah, I have six hours to braise) and the often-arduous task of kitchen and meal prep. Who has the energy? And is the alternative then "fast" food? It doesn't need to be. Life is busy. I get that. We need food, fast. But we also want something that is wholesome, delicious, easy to prepare and appealing to the whole family and, as much as possible, can be made in 30 minutes or less. Too big an ask? Heck NO!

My strategy is simple: I don't meal plan. I eat what I want to eat, when I want to eat it, because deciding what to eat for Thursday's dinner on Monday morning doesn't make sense to me. Maybe I'll want pasta, or grilled fish, or a hearty salad. Maybe I'll see a picture of a roast chicken thigh on Instagram and now I just NEED roast chicken. I want to be free of a plan and I want to cook what I crave. Some of you might break out into a sweat just imagining the anxiety this non-plan plan might induce, but let me tell you, this is achievable. I understand that we could all use a cheat sheet on our quest for happier, fuller lives. I want that cheat sheet and those tried-and-true shortcuts that really go the distance. But I also want to embrace the messy mistakes that turn into memorable moments.

Spontaneity is possible, even during the weekday crunch. My first recommendation to achieve this is to have a kitchen that is always stocked with the right basics, a combination of fresh produce and shelf-stable items. If you've got the right pieces, the opportunities for mixing and matching are endless. I believe that less is more, and a truly delicious meal doesn't really need more than a handful of ingredients, most of which are things kicking around your kitchen already.

You'll begin to notice pretty quickly that I favor punchy, bold flavors (hi vinegar, salt, lemons, fresh herbs, capers, fish sauce, tangy yogurt, Parm) that can do wonders for any simple dish. All of my recipes are meant to inspire creativity and spontaneity in the kitchen. I use simple methods to create deliciously straightforward dishes that are fun to cook, all while celebrating seasonal produce and quality products and ingredients. Gathering together over good food is one of life's greatest joys, and you will find my favorite entertaining tips peppered throughout the chapters. It's all meant to be fun, not stressful.

And the most important rule of thumb when cooking? Remember why you're doing it. And who you're doing it for. We've not yet experienced a time when cooking at home and eating together has been more fulfilling. We're staying in, we're experimenting, we're having fun with food.

Everything that you find in *Conveniently Delicious* is meant to bring you joy, comfort, amusement and perhaps a little spark of "huh—I hadn't thought of that." As you read, know that my aim is to leave you feeling a little lighter about mealtimes than when you started . . . even if most of the time I'm talking about how to make you feel full.

A NOTE ON PANTRY STAPLES
AND KITCHEN TOOLS

I'm not one of those people whose pantries are filled with Lucite containers with the names of each ingredient lovingly scribed in chalk paint on the front. I'm more of a mismatched can, open box, jumbled spice drawer type of person. Mine is a pantry that gets used. Although I sometimes wish it could resemble more Martha and less mayhem, I like that my pantry works well, hard and often.

Many cookbooks contain a laundry list of ingredients and tools. Very helpful for a novice cook setting up their kitchen, but in recent years, I've found that the vast majority of cookbook buyers and readers already love to cook and likely (or sort of) know their way around a kitchen. They've got their favorites already—the oils, vinegars, mustards, spices. With this book, I'm assuming that you're one of those kinds of cooks, someone who has a basic pantry and tool setup already. If you stumble on a recipe that requires something you don't have, I guarantee that it'll be a max of three or four items and not a Costco run.

I still cook and write recipes with the mentality I had in my 20s, living in New York. If an ingredient wasn't available at my bodega around the corner, I wouldn't make the recipe. Think: your common spices, oils, condiments, crackers, canned beans, etc. You're not going to find puntarella, dukkah and pickled herring in this book, not because I don't love them, but because my style goes for convenience just as much as delicious.

When it comes to storing shelf-stable items, use your own logic to sort them. I keep my dried fruits and nuts together with things like chips, pretzels, crackers and other snacking items. Some people put their nuts and dried fruits with granolas and cereals. Different strokes for different folks. Do what feels intuitive to you and work with your kitchen layout.

Same goes for equipment and tools. Most professional kitchens are stocked with cheap aluminum pans and throwaway knives (I know this from years of experience). They make it work. I'm all for a high-quality Dutch oven and a solid chef's knife, but you won't find a sous vide circulator in my kitchen. Or a steam oven. Or a matching set of copper pots and pans or even a super-fancy stove. It's just not necessary. And not a single recipe in this book requires anything of the sort.

My goal in not prescribing a huge grocery or equipment list isn't to make you feel like you're on your own. Rather, it's to empower you, to show you that no matter what kind of kitchen you have, amazing recipes are within your reach. You can do this. I'll show you how.

PEOPLE LAUGHING. MUSIC. A CORK POPPING. THE CLINK OF ICE. SOMETHING GOOD TO EAT.

The alchemy of a good night.

Let me be clear: how to host a good night is 18% about the food and 82% about everything else. What is everything else? It's making people feel comfortable as soon as they enter the door (I highly recommend a stiff cocktail off the bat). It's connecting people with common interests. It's good lighting (turn off the overheads—low-lit lamps and candles only). It's music that's fun and sexy and changes with the tempo of the evening. It's a simple and delicious (but not perfect) meal. It's moving from one room to the next (or switching up table-mates halfway through dinner). It's an element of surprise (adult milkshakes for dessert? Why not?). It's an opportunity to create a memorable night. One that you'll talk about years later.

The following pages share my top tips.

1.
GET INSPIRED

I like setting a loose theme for an evening. It allows me to get creative within a smaller orbit and makes decision-making easier. For example: For a dinner party, I might decide to channel my latest trip to Italy. So that means spritzes for cocktails (and by spritz I'm talking about anything boozy and sparkly over a ton of ice), room-temp nibbles (two to three nice cured meats, olives, some higher-quality plain potato chips, toasted bread rubbed with garlic and olive oil, and some nice hunks of Parm) and then a simple salad like Radicchio, Orange & Pistachio Salad (p. 37) followed by Chicken Puttanesca-Style (p. 184). Stick within one genre and you'll simplify the whole affair and avoid having to buy your groceries at multiple locations.

2.
ENJOY YOUR NIGHT

I try to prepare as much as possible before guests arrive, without going too overboard. I put on some music, pour myself a tea (or a glass of wine, depending on the time) and get to prepping. I set the table, which is a task far easier and faster done without your guests watching, prep any elements of the meal that I can do ahead of time, and do a quick tidy-up. When guests arrive, I am ideally just a few small tasks away from the finished meal hitting the table.

Now for the ongoing debate: to invite the help of guests or not? My opinion? *Absolutely*. They want it, you want it, why do the song and dance to avoid it? It's a win-win. The key is the *type* of help you assign. I often leave a few "wine tasks" (things that can be done with a glass of wine in hand or nearby—think: shelling peas, folding napkins, etc.)—unfinished to accommodate the inevitable offerings of help that unfold upon arrival. Greet your guests with a cocktail and some nibbles, and after the initial catch-up, when a few guests meander into the kitchen, have some tasks ready to go that won't leave them dirty, hot or resentful. Keep them away from the stove, happily seated nearby so the conversation flows and it is an extension of the party. Also, do not exclude kids from the fun! I leave certain jobs for my boys, like shucking corn and tip-and-tailing green beans. Those tasks are perfect for little hands and the boys love getting into the mix. I also love to outsource, and that goes for help in the kitchen as well. Whether it be someone from an agency or my neighbor's 16-year-old looking for some extra pocket money, I often seek assistance for cleanup purposes when hosting larger parties. No shame in that game!

I think the days of the "traditional dinner party" are somewhat numbered. Cocktails in the living room followed by a plated dinner in the dining room feels stuffy and doesn't allow for mingling. I like my guests to move around and talk to as many people as possible. This means having drinks in the living room and the kitchen! Set up ice buckets and open bottles of wine. The first thing I tell people when they enter the house is that "it's a serve-yourself evening." Don't expect me to fill your glass, just grab an open bottle and pour for yourself whenever you like.

3.
PARTY
IN A
BOX

For those last-minute, spontaneous shindigs that you truly can't plan for and that happen at least once or twice every summer, I keep a box or corner of the pantry full of party necessities ready to go. This includes shelf-stable food like tinned fish, preserves, crackers, chips and cornichons, but it also contains games (cards, dice), party supplies (cocktail napkins, swizzle sticks) and cocktail accoutrements (bitters, syrups). It's a great way to keep things organized and a way to use up treasures from your travels. That can of tomato-preserved sardines you bought in Portugal? Pop it in there! The goal is to gather items that are simple to prepare and lead to a stress-free impromptu gathering as long, hot summer afternoons melt into evenings and beyond.

4.
ADD AN
ELEMENT
OF
SURPRISE

Just to keep things fresh and fun, I like to throw one curveball into the evening. To give you context, my favorite annual party is my holiday Champagne & Hot Wings fete, the ultimate in classy/crassy shindiggery. That is an extreme example, but surprising your guests with something playful and unexpected adds a touch of whimsy to any gathering and can be as simple (and inexpensive) as you wish. Stumped on what to serve for dessert for a dinner party in the middle of summer? A giant platter of Klondike bars is the answer. Feeling blah about your space? Create a showstopping charcuterie display by grabbing a six-foot-long board from the lumberyard and dressing it to the nines (just make sure to put a food-safe barrier between the board and the food). Shake up the place-card game by assigning each guest a Pez dispenser and having them guess which one they are (this always makes for lively conversation). Or why not make a DIY gin and tonic bar with tons of garnishes and mixers? (I like cucumber and cracked black pepper, personally.) The best thing you can do is have fun with it!

NIBBLES

SOMETIMES I FEEL SILLY SAYING "FOOLPROOF."

Like, if you're cooking in the first place, you're already not a fool. But sometimes a recipe is just so damn easy that you can practically do it with your eyes closed—and only a fool would do that, right? Many of the recipes here, in fact, require no cooking at all. It's assembly cooking at its finest. Crunchy fresh veg, sweet and savory cheeses and dips, bright acids—this is how I snack.

Whether you're hosting a crowd or need a snack while cooking (because snacking while cooking is *the best*), what follows is a series of easy, delicious bites that may take you one step out of your cut veg and hummus rotation. Don't get me wrong, I love cut veg and hummus, but if you have time to chop some veggies, you likely have time to try some of these. A bite, a nibble, a snack . . . a delight.

SESAME HONEY HALLOUMI

SERVES 4

One 6–8 oz block halloumi cheese

2 Tbsp white sesame seeds

2 Tbsp olive oil

2–3 Tbsp liquid honey

Black pepper, to taste

Halloumi—that super-salty, squeaky block of cheese that can be sliced and pan-fried without melting—is one of life's greatest snacking pleasures. I talk a lot about salty-sweet things in this book, and this ingredient might characterize that balance the most. Ready in a "flash of the pan," the halloumi gets cut into squares and drizzled with honey, some sesame seeds and a good amount of pepper. It really couldn't be easier. Even at room temperature, they are still tasty.

Cut the halloumi in ¼-inch slices (you should end up with about 12–14 pieces total). Place the slices on paper towels and blot away any moisture.

Heat a nonstick skillet on high. Add the sesame seeds to the dry pan and toast for about 1 minute, being careful not to burn them. Remove from the pan and set aside.

In the same pan, add the olive oil, immediately followed by the halloumi. Fry for about 1 minute per side, checking throughout to make sure the cheese is browning well. The halloumi will not melt and will hold its shape throughout cooking.

Place the halloumi on a serving plate. Drizzle with the honey, then top with the sesame seeds and black pepper. Serve right away while still hot.

HOUSE NUTS

MAKES 2 CUPS

2 cups blanched (skinless) almonds

2 Tbsp finely chopped rosemary leaves

2 tsp flaky sea salt

½ tsp chili flakes

½ cup golden raisins

1 Tbsp olive oil

1 Tbsp brown sugar

Every home needs a "house nut" that can be pulled out for last-minute entertaining reasons (cue the joke about Uncle Larry). Something a little more exciting than a bowl of salted cashews. A batch of these goodies will probably last you two hosting situations. Store them in a container in the pantry or send them off as gifts— they are such a treat. The technique here is based on the classic mid-90s snack made famous at Danny Meyer's Union Square Cafe. Salty-sweet toasted nuts served with a heavy pour of white wine on the side. Take me back to the time of sitting at a crowded New York bar any day of the week.

Preheat the oven to 350°F and line a baking sheet with parchment paper.

Toast the almonds on the baking sheet for 10 minutes, until very lightly browned and fragrant.

Meanwhile, in a mixing bowl, combine the chopped rosemary, salt, chili flakes, raisins and olive oil. Pour the hot nuts over the mixture and toss to coat. Sprinkle the brown sugar overtop and toss again. Sprinkling the sugar at the last minute helps prevent clumping, but if you see this happening, use the back of a spoon to break it up. The nuts will keep in a sealed container in the pantry for up to 1 month.

NOTE
Blanched almonds are usually found in the baking section of the supermarket.

GRILLED ASPARAGUS WITH TONNATO & CHILI

SERVES 4

2 bunches asparagus, bottoms trimmed

2 Tbsp + ¼ cup olive oil, divided

½ tsp kosher salt

¼ tsp black pepper

Two 5 oz cans Italian tuna in oil, drained

½ cup mayonnaise

3 Tbsp lemon juice + wedges for serving

½ tsp chili flakes

Tonnato sauce, on paper, seems, well, not very sexy. On the taste buds, however, it's something else entirely. You may have encountered tonnato sauce with its most common companion, chilled slices of veal, in vitello tonnato, which is a traditional Italian dish often served at lunch. Here, I've paired it with lightly grilled asparagus for dipping. Think of it as a new take on crudité with dip. A little more complex and a whole lot more interesting. You'll end up with more dip than you need. It's excellent with any crunchy fresh veg, like radish or fennel, and will keep in the fridge for up to 5 days.

Preheat your grill (or a grill pan) to high.

Toss the trimmed asparagus with 2 tablespoons of olive oil and the salt and pepper. Grill for 2–3 minutes per side, until the asparagus is bright green and charred in some areas. Don't overcook; you want the asparagus to still be "dippable."

Place the tuna, mayonnaise and lemon juice in a high-speed blender. With the motor on, drizzle in the remaining ¼ cup olive oil until incorporated and the mixture is very smooth. Taste for seasoning and add salt if needed. Pour into a small bowl.

Place the asparagus on a platter alongside the bowl of tonnato. Sprinkle the asparagus with chili flakes and garnish with lemon wedges.

MAKE AHEAD
The tonnato sauce can be made up to 5 days in advance.

CHICKPEA FLOUR BLINIS WITH ROASTED GRAPE TOMATOES, BURRATA & BASIL PESTO

SERVES 6

2 cups grape tomatoes

5 Tbsp olive oil, divided

1 Tbsp balsamic vinegar

1 tsp kosher salt, divided

1 cup chickpea flour

¼ tsp black pepper

½ ball (4 oz) burrata or buffalo mozzarella, torn into 1-inch pieces

3 Tbsp good-quality store-bought basil pesto

½ cup arugula

Zest of 1 lemon

I make chickpea flour pancakes a lot in my house, even as a sub for pizza crust when I make them dinner plate–size. Top them with any ingredients you like (Italian tuna, arugula and tomatoes for me). Here, I've made mini versions perfect for holding with one hand and drinking with the other. They don't have to be served hot, so they're an ideal entertaining snack. I like putting these out on a large board to serve—it's a little more casual and leaves your hands free for mixing drinks and eating.

Preheat the oven to 375°F.

In a small baking dish, toss the tomatoes with 1 tablespoon of olive oil, the balsamic vinegar and ½ teaspoon kosher salt. Bake until the tomatoes have blistered and popped, about 15 minutes.

In a bowl, whisk together the chickpea flour, 1 cup water, 1 tablespoon of olive oil, the remaining ½ teaspoon kosher salt and the black pepper, until smooth. Set aside for a minimum of 5 minutes to rest.

In a large nonstick skillet over medium-high heat, heat 1 tablespoon of olive oil. Ladle the chickpea batter into four pancakes, about 2 inches across. Fry for 2–3 minutes, or until bubbles appear. Flip and continue to cook for 2–3 minutes more, until golden brown. Repeat with the remaining olive oil and batter. Transfer the cooked pancakes to a large platter.

Place a piece of burrata on top of each pancake. Add one or two tomatoes and drizzle with pesto. Sprinkle with a few choice leaves of arugula and some lemon zest.

MAKE AHEAD

Roasted tomatoes can be made 2 days in advance and brought to room temperature before serving. The batter can be made up to 1 hour in advance and left out at room temperature.

OLIVE & THYME BAKED FETA WITH HONEY

SERVES 6–8

1 lb good-quality sheep's milk feta

¾ cup pitted black and green olives

6 sprigs thyme

2 sprigs rosemary

1 lemon, zest removed in strips with a vegetable peeler

3 Tbsp olive oil

2 Tbsp honey

Kosher salt and black pepper, to taste

1 loaf crusty bread or pita wedges, for serving

This is the antithesis of a fussy little canapé. Picture it. You place a beautiful dish of bubbling warm feta down on the coffee table. The smell of herbs and lemon permeate the air. It's rustic and inviting. Your guests think you are a kitchen genius. Little do they know you just threw a brick of cheese in the oven and voilà! Well, there's a little more to it than that, but we're close. Feta isn't a cheese you often think to warm up, but when you do, it becomes creamy and spreadable. Don't be too precious about how the feta is laid out in the baking dish. It can be slightly overlapping and different heights. Do serve this immediately out of the oven, as the cheese can begin to harden as it cools. It's just as delicious, but more crumbly.

Preheat the oven to 400°F.

Slice the feta to fit in the bottom of a small or medium-sized ovenproof baking dish. Scatter the olives over and around the feta. Arrange the thyme and rosemary sprigs and lemon zest strips on top of the feta. Drizzle the olive oil over the herbs and feta, ensuring the herbs are well coated so they don't burn.

Bake the feta for 15 minutes, until it begins to melt slightly. Remove from the oven and drizzle the honey overtop. Season with a pinch of salt and a good crack of black pepper. Serve warm with crusty bread or wedges of pita.

MAKE AHEAD
Assemble the entire dish up to the day before and refrigerate covered in plastic wrap. Pop in the oven right before serving.

QUICK-PICKLED FENNEL WITH OLIVES, ORANGE & CHILI

SERVES 4–6

1 large bulb fennel

3 Tbsp red wine vinegar

1 tsp finely chopped rosemary leaves

1 Tbsp olive oil

¼ tsp chili flakes

½ tsp kosher salt

½ cup Calatrava or green olives

1 tsp orange zest + 3–4 zest strips removed with a vegetable peeler

I love fennel. Shaved, sliced, in chunks, roasted and raw. It can do it all. This is a great snack served alongside some cured meats and grilled bread for more of an antipasto-style nibbles platter, but it can also be made simply without the olives for when I want something to snack on while I'm cooking (which is always). Don't slice the fennel too thinly here—it should be stiff enough to pick up with your fingers. Definitely think about serving a Spritz Royale with this (Campari, prosecco and orange). Very effortlessly Italian, very chic.

Trim the stalk off the fennel and cut the bulb in half vertically. Remove the core of the fennel by cutting it out at the base in a V-shape. Slice the fennel lengthwise into ¼- or ½-inch pieces. Place the fennel in a large bowl and toss with the vinegar, rosemary, olive oil, chili flakes and salt. Let sit for a minimum of 10 minutes before draining the excess vinegar.

Toss in the olives and orange zest and strips before serving.

LABNEH WITH BURSTED TOMATOES & DILL

SERVES 4–6

2 cups cherry tomatoes (about 10–12)

2 Tbsp balsamic vinegar

2 Tbsp olive oil + more for drizzling

½ tsp kosher salt

Black pepper, to taste

1 cup labneh

1 Tbsp finely chopped dill

1 Tbsp finely chopped chives or green onions

Toasted flatbread or naan, for serving

I like to think that all the recipes in this book, and in this chapter especially, are super easy to pull off, but this one is next-level easy. A handful of ingredients, served simply. Roasting tomatoes, especially in the winter when they're not at their peak, intensifies their flavor and boosts their sweetness. Serve them warm atop the cool labneh with some pita or toast and you're in for a real treat. If you can't find labneh, use Greek yogurt with the highest fat content available (the closest comparison is 10%).

Preheat the oven to 450°F.

Place the tomatoes in a small ovenproof baking dish and toss with the balsamic vinegar, olive oil, salt and pepper. Roast for 15 minutes, until the tomatoes have burst and wilted slightly.

Spread the labneh in a shallow bowl, making large swoops with the back of a spoon. Spoon the tomatoes and pan juices over the labneh. Sprinkle with the herbs and drizzle with olive oil.

Serve with toasted flatbread or naan.

CAULIFLOWER TAHINI DIP

SERVES 6

1 medium head cauliflower, cut into florets

4 medium cloves garlic, skin removed

3 Tbsp + ¼ cup olive oil, divided, + more for drizzling

1 tsp kosher salt

Black pepper, to taste

⅓ cup tahini

3 Tbsp lemon juice (about 1 lemon)

¼ tsp sweet paprika

Roasting cauliflower until tender and slightly brown and then whipping it with roasted garlic, tahini and lemon makes for the absolute creamiest and delicious spread or dip. An undeniable upgrade from hummus, it's sweeter and silkier and is amazing when served with the obvious, fresh vegetables and grilled or toasted pita.

Preheat the oven to 425°F and line a baking sheet with parchment paper.

Toss the cauliflower and garlic cloves with 3 tablespoons of olive oil and roast on the lined baking sheet for 30 minutes, until the cauliflower has started to brown and the garlic is soft.

Remove the cauliflower and garlic from the oven and place in a high-speed blender. Pour in the remaining ¼ cup of olive oil, salt, pepper, tahini and lemon juice. Blend on medium speed, scraping down the bowl after 30 seconds. Increase the speed to high and blend for 1–2 minutes, until very smooth. Add 1–2 tablespoons of water if you want a thinner consistency.

Scoop the dip into a wide-mouth serving bowl and swirl with the back of a spoon. Drizzle with a little olive oil and a sprinkling of the sweet paprika.

MAKE AHEAD
The dip can be made up to 3 days in advance and refrigerated.

AVOCADO YOGURT CREMA WITH ICED CRUDITÉ

SERVES 6

6 breakfast radishes

2 avocados, roughly chopped

¾ cup plain Greek yogurt (not 0% fat)

1 Tbsp finely chopped chives

1 Tbsp finely chopped cilantro

¼ cup lime juice

½ tsp chili flakes

1 tsp kosher salt

1 tsp poppy seeds or black sesame seeds

Carrots, fennel, radishes and sugar snap peas, for serving

A cool and creamy dip with some crispy veggies and little toasts is a classic snacking scenario, but we're gaining extra presentation points here with radish petals. Aside from radishes, putting any shaved veg in ice water for about 15 minutes does wonders—it curls them and makes them extra crunchy. Put that mandoline to use and get an ice bath ready—it's so worth the added step. The crema would be incredible on tacos or as a dip for quesadillas; try it anywhere you would use a creamy topping or dip.

Prepare an ice bath. Using a mandoline, shave the radishes lengthwise as thin as possible. Place the radishes in the ice bath—this will turn them translucent and slightly curl them so they resemble flower petals.

Place the avocados, Greek yogurt, chives, cilantro, lime juice, chili flakes and salt in a high-speed blender. Blend on medium-high until smooth, scraping down the sides of the blender one or two times in between. The spread should be silky-smooth and creamy.

Spoon the dip into a bowl and place the radish petals in a pretty pattern overtop. Sprinkle poppy seeds over one half of the dip. Serve with carrots, fennel, radishes and sugar snap peas over crushed ice.

SALADS
& SOUPS

IF YOU ASKED ME TO EAT ONE THING

for the rest of my life, it would be a salad. (Sure, the salad may accompany a veal scallopini or some fried cheese, but that's my answer and I'm sticking to it.)

In this chapter I'm offering up salads as sides, salads as full meals, salads for salad fanatics (that's me!) and non-salad-eaters alike (that's my kids!). Of course, I focus on fresh, seasonal vegetables wherever I can, but I also welcome some peak seasonal fruits into the mix. Note: fruit in salads, not fruit salads.

Try interchanging the dressing or making double batches of it to keep in the fridge to last the week. I tend to go heavier on the acid component of my dressings, upping the ratio of juice or vinegar to oil closer to one-third or two-thirds acid to oil.

And speaking of ratios, a good salad needs equal parts crunch (a nut or crouton), bitter (lemon, vinegar), sweet (fruit, honey, dried fruit) and fresh (that's your cue, lettuce). That's just salad math.

And what is a salad chapter without soup? Like jam to peanut butter, like eggs to bacon . . . like soup to salad. You'll find a number of combinations here that might surprise you or hearken back to a meal you've had once before. Now it's time to make it at home.

RADICCHIO, ORANGE & PISTACHIO SALAD

SERVES 6

SALAD

2 navel or blood oranges

2 heads radicchio

¼ red onion, thinly sliced in half-moons, soaked in cold water for 10 minutes

¼ cup salted pistachios, roughly chopped

½ cup (4 oz) crumbled blue cheese

VINAIGRETTE

2 Tbsp red wine vinegar

1 Tbsp honey

1 tsp kosher salt + more to taste

Black pepper, to taste

¼ cup olive oil + more for drizzling

This salad . . . you could write an art history thesis on this one. The complementary colors, the textures, the juxtaposition of salty, sweet, bitter and sour. Those moody blues! She's a work of art. A great salad for fall and winter months, I'd pair it with a sliced grilled steak to make it a fully composed meal. Soaking the red onions in cold water takes the bite out of them and mellows their flavor. I recommend doing this for any dish that requires raw onions, unless you like onion breath, so in that instance, it's up to you. If you don't have blue cheese, use goat, and you can also sub almonds for the pistachios. (She may be pretty, but fussy she is not.)

Cut off the top and bottom ends of the oranges and run the knife along the sides of the oranges between the flesh and skin to remove the skin and pith. Slice the oranges in ¼-inch thick rounds.

Quarter the radicchio heads and separate the leaves by hand.

To make the vinaigrette, in a large mixing bowl, stir together the red wine vinegar, honey, salt, pepper and ¼ cup olive oil. Add the radicchio to the bowl and toss well.

Place the dressed radicchio on a platter and tuck the orange slices in and around the radicchio. Drain the red onions, pat dry with paper towels and scatter overtop, followed by the pistachios and the crumbled blue cheese.

Finish with an extra drizzle of olive oil, salt and pepper.

APPLE, CHEDDAR, CELERY & KALE SALAD

SERVES 6

My mom used to serve an apple and cheddar sandwich on raisin-walnut bread at the ACE Bakery Cafe, and it was a favorite of mine for years. I turned that sandwich into a hearty salad here, and it's one of the few salads my own kids will consume with enthusiasm. This may just be the one that converts those non-salad-eating kids once and for all. Leave the walnuts out if you're not into them, but someone once told me that eating foods that look like brains is good for your brain, and kids love stories about brains, so we're rolling with it.

SALAD

¾ cup raw walnuts

6 stalks celery + a handful of leaves

2 Pink Lady, Gala or Ambrosia apples

3 cups finely chopped black kale

¾ cup shaved white cheddar, divided (see note)

VINAIGRETTE

1 Tbsp Dijon mustard

2 Tbsp lemon juice

1 Tbsp apple cider vinegar

½ tsp finely grated garlic

1 Tbsp honey

1 tsp kosher salt + more to taste

Black pepper, to taste

⅓ cup olive oil

Preheat the oven to 350°F and line a baking sheet with parchment paper. Place the walnuts on the baking sheet. Bake for 5 minutes until slightly golden and fragrant. Cool slightly and roughly chop.

Slice the celery stalks on a diagonal, about ¼ inch thick. Quarter each apple, remove the core and slice into half-moon shapes as thinly as possible. Place the sliced celery, celery leaves and apples in a large serving bowl along with the toasted walnuts and kale. Add half of the cheddar.

To make the vinaigrette, in a small bowl, whisk together the Dijon, lemon juice, vinegar, garlic, honey, salt and pepper. Slowly drizzle in the olive oil, continually whisking, until combined.

Pour the vinaigrette over the salad and toss. To serve, top with the remaining cheddar and a little more salt and pepper.

NOTE

Shave your cheddar cheese with a cheese planer or very carefully with a sharp knife. You want large shards, not small gratings.

PLUM, HAZELNUT, FRISÉE, SHALLOT & PARM SALAD

SERVES 4

You might be seeing a trend with my salads in that I really like adding fruit to them. A hint of sweetness and a touch of color are great for balance. Have you ever tried a plum with a hazelnut in one bite? So damn good. Red plums are my favorite here, but yellow, purple or golden plums work as well. I prefer this served on a platter as opposed to a bowl, as the heavier ingredients can sink to the bottom and get lost. Let those plums shine.

SALAD

3 plums, not too ripe

½ cup hazelnuts

1 large frisée lettuce head, roughly chopped (about 4 cups)

1 small shallot, sliced very thinly into rounds

½ cup shaved Parmigiano-Reggiano (see note)

VINAIGRETTE

1 Tbsp Dijon mustard

2 Tbsp lemon juice

1 Tbsp balsamic vinegar

½ tsp finely grated garlic

1 Tbsp honey

1 tsp kosher salt

Black pepper, to taste

⅓ cup olive oil

Preheat the oven to 375°F and line a baking sheet with parchment paper.

Slice the plums into ¼-inch wedges. If the pits are hard to remove, sometimes the easiest way to do this is by cutting the "cheeks" off the plums and slicing them cut side down on a cutting board.

Put the hazelnuts on the lined baking sheet. Toast in the oven for 8–10 minutes, keeping a close eye to prevent burning. The skin on the hazelnuts will begin to crack and turn a very dark brown. Remove from the oven and place the nuts in the middle of a clean dishcloth. Gather the edges of the dishcloth and rub the hazelnuts vigorously to remove the skin. Discard the papery skins and place the hazelnuts on a cutting board. Carefully chop the hazelnuts (so they don't fly all over your kitchen) until they are roughly quartered.

Place the roughly chopped frisée in a large shallow serving bowl and scatter with the shallots and sliced plums.

To make the vinaigrette, in a small bowl, whisk together the Dijon, lemon juice, balsamic vinegar, garlic, honey, salt and pepper. Slowly drizzle in the olive oil, continually whisking until combined.

Spoon the vinaigrette over the frisée, shallots and plums. Scatter the hazelnuts and Parmigiano overtop, and serve. The salad will toss itself when you spoon it out onto people's plates.

NOTE
Shave your Parmigiano cheese with a cheese planer or very carefully with a sharp knife. You want large shards, not small gratings.

MAKE AHEAD
Toast and skin the hazelnuts up to 1 week beforehand and keep in the fridge.

NECTARINE, BABY GEM, FRIED ALMOND & FETA SALAD

SERVES 4

SALAD

1 Tbsp olive oil

⅓ cup blanched (skinless) almonds

Kosher salt, to taste

2 ripe but firm nectarines

4 heads baby gem lettuce, cleaned and leaves separated, or 2–3 heads regular romaine, outer leaves removed

½ cup crumbled feta

VINAIGRETTE

1 Tbsp Dijon mustard

1 Tbsp finely chopped fresh mint

½ tsp finely grated garlic

2 Tbsp lemon juice

1 Tbsp red wine vinegar

Kosher salt and black pepper, to taste

⅓ cup olive oil

Baby gem lettuce has a way of managing a dressing so perfectly, it really is a little hero of a leafy green. It's delicate in flavor but hearty in composition, so it can handle being dressed beforehand without wilting, which makes it a perfect addition to any backyard barbecue. You can even bring this one already dressed (gasp!) to a party, and it will hold up even as the cocktails have been served and the host fiddles with the playlist. If you can't find baby gem, you can substitute with romaine—just remove the outer darker leaves and save those for tomorrow night's Caesar salad. Use raw almonds here if you can't find blanched (often found in the baking section), and don't get tripped up if nectarines aren't on the menu. Any stone fruit (a peach, a plum) will work beautifully.

In a small skillet over medium heat, heat 1 tablespoon olive oil. Add the almonds and allow them to brown for about 1 minute before stirring. Then stir occasionally for the next 1–2 minutes, and keep a close eye to avoid any burning. Once the nuts are toasted and brown, remove the pan from the heat and sprinkle with salt. Allow to cool before roughly chopping.

Slice the nectarines in half and remove the pit. You might need to use a paring knife to cut around the pit to remove it. Cut the nectarines into half-moon shapes as thinly as possible.

To make the vinaigrette, in a small bowl, whisk together the Dijon, mint, garlic, lemon juice, vinegar, salt and pepper until the salt has dissolved. Slowly drizzle in ⅓ cup olive oil and continue whisking until combined.

Scatter the leaves of baby gem in a shallow bowl. Toss with two-thirds of the vinaigrette. Top with the nectarines, feta and fried almonds. Drizzle with a couple more spoonfuls of vinaigrette and serve.

RADISH & BUTTER LETTUCE SALAD WITH YOGURT DRESSING & SEEDS

SERVES 4–6

I never thought I'd be the person who topped her salad with seeds, but here we are. They give a great crunchy texture and subtle flavor and they make a salad even more healthy and delicious—though this one doesn't need it. I like to imagine that Ottolenghi popped by and made me this herby, tangy salad. We'd pair it with a grilled or poached salmon and talk about the benefits of sumac, and all would be right in the world.

SALAD

1 bunch (about 6–8) radishes, trimmed

1 large head butter or Boston lettuce, washed and leaves separated

¼ cup tarragon leaves, roughly chopped

2 Tbsp minced chives

1½ tsp poppy seeds

1½ tsp white sesame seeds

DRESSING

½ cup plain 2% yogurt (see note)

2 Tbsp apple cider vinegar

2 Tbsp olive oil

¾ tsp kosher salt

¼ tsp black pepper

Using a mandoline or very sharp knife, slice the radishes as thinly as possible and place in an ice bath.

To make the dressing, in a bowl, whisk together the yogurt, vinegar, olive oil, salt and pepper. Set aside.

When ready to serve, remove the radishes from the ice bath and dry thoroughly with paper towels. Place the whole butter lettuce leaves (tear them slightly if you wish), tarragon, chives and half the radishes into a large bowl. Using your hands, toss with half of the vinaigrette (butter lettuce can bruise very easily, so using your hands to toss lowers this risk). Add more dressing if needed. Scatter the dressed lettuce and herbs over a large platter.

Sprinkle with poppy and sesame seeds and the remaining radish slices and serve immediately.

NOTE
I can't remember the last time I bought regular plain old yogurt instead of Greek, but this recipe needs it. Greek is too thick.

MAKE AHEAD
Make the vinaigrette up to 2 days in advance. For the salad, clean the lettuce the day before. Slice the radishes and keep in cold water in the fridge for up to 1 day.

ROASTED PEPPER & PEACH SALAD WITH SOURDOUGH CROUTONS

SERVES 6

This is an impressive showstopper of a salad, but summer is really when you want to show it off. I make this salad at least once a week when peaches are in season, and no matter who is on the receiving end of it, mouthfuls of "mmmm" inevitably punctuate every bite. I would usually recommend taking a shortcut and buying roasted red peppers, but they are just too limp and stringy here. You want the bite of those freshly grilled peppers. The fresh mint and basil are more than supporting players here; they play a big part in texture and flavor, so make sure they aren't limp or wilting.

SALAD

4 large red bell peppers

½ red onion

Three 1-inch-thick slices sourdough boule

3 large peaches, cut in ¼-inch slices

½ cup tightly packed mint leaves, roughly torn

½ cup tightly packed basil leaves, roughly torn

One 9 oz ball buffalo mozzarella

Kosher salt and black pepper, to taste

VINAIGRETTE

1 Tbsp Dijon mustard

1 tsp grated garlic

Juice of 1 lemon

1 Tbsp red wine vinegar

½ tsp kosher salt

¼ tsp black pepper

½ cup olive oil

On a hot barbecue grill, directly on the flame of your gas burner, or under the oven broiler (choices!), char the peppers for a few minutes on each side, until the skin is blackened on all sides.

Meanwhile, thinly slice the red onion into half-moons and soak them in cold water for 10 minutes. This takes the oniony bite out of them and mellows the flavor.

Once the peppers are charred, transfer them to a large bowl, cover with a clean dishcloth and allow them to steam for 5 minutes. Once the peppers are cool enough to touch, peel the skin from them using your fingers or a small paring knife. Remove the stems and the seeds and cut in ½-inch slices.

On the same grill, burner or broiler, toast the bread until brown and charred in some spots. Once cool to the touch, tear into large croutons. The bread will still be soft in the interior.

To make the vinaigrette, in a small bowl, whisk together the Dijon, garlic, lemon juice, vinegar, salt and pepper until the salt has dissolved. Slowly drizzle in the olive oil and continue whisking.

Remove the red onions from the water and pat dry with paper towels. Place the cut peppers, peaches, onions and croutons in a large bowl and toss with the vinaigrette, allowing to sit for 5 minutes. Add the herbs and gently toss to coat.

Arrange on a large platter, scatter with torn pieces of mozzarella and season with more salt and pepper to finish.

GRILLED CAESAR SALAD WITH CASHEW DRESSING & SWEET POTATO CROUTONS

SERVES 4

I'm fully aware, thank you, that it's risky to mess with a good thing. And there is definitely more than one risk-taking moment happening here. We're grilling the lettuce to deepen the flavor, we're making a dressing with creamy cashews instead of oil and eggs, and we're roasting sweet potatoes into crisp, sweet and salty morsels. It's a Caesar salad that went on a Palm Springs wellness retreat and has come back refreshed and *maybe* better than before. I love this dressing on a multitude of salads and even just drizzled on roasted veggies. Make double and store it in the fridge for up to 1 week.

DRESSING

½ tsp grated garlic

2 Tbsp apple cider vinegar

¼ cup olive oil

½ cup unsalted cashews

1 tsp kosher salt

¼ tsp black pepper

CROUTONS

1 small to medium sweet potato

2 tsp olive oil

1 tsp harissa paste or ½ tsp smoked paprika

¼ tsp kosher salt

SALAD

2 large heads romaine lettuce, sliced in half lengthwise

Lemon wedges, for serving

Preheat the oven to 350°F and line a baking sheet with parchment paper.

For the dressing, place the garlic, vinegar, olive oil, cashews, salt, pepper and ¼ cup water in a food processor or blender. Blend on medium speed, scraping down as necessary, until very smooth and creamy. Add more water if needed to achieve a liquid honey consistency.

For the croutons, scrub the skin of the sweet potato and cut in ½-inch cubes. Place the sweet potatoes on the prepared baking sheet and toss with the olive oil, harissa and salt. Bake for 20–25 minutes, until golden brown around the edges. Allow to cool slightly.

For the salad, heat a grill pan or barbecue on high for 4–5 minutes. The pan or grill must be extremely hot for the lettuce to char quickly but not wilt. Place the lettuce in the pan or on the grill, cut side down, and grill for 1 minute, or until it has nice dark grill marks. Only grill on one side.

Place the lettuce in a large serving bowl and drizzle liberally with the dressing. Scatter with the sweet potato croutons and garnish with lemon wedges.

FENNEL & ASIAN PEAR SLAW

SERVES 4

Slaw is always a good idea when paired with fried or rich foods, as it cuts the fat. This one is a versatile side slaw that pairs well with any meat (try it with the Pork Tonkatsu on p. 196 and see what I mean). If you can't find an Asian pear, a firm Bartlett or Bosc pear is a good substitute. Be sure to core your fennel before slicing, as the core is very tough and hard to digest. And finally, keep the slaw very cold before serving, and only toss it at the last minute, as it is very delicate. Just the thing your hefty fried pork needs.

SALAD

1 bulb fennel

¼ head purple cabbage

1 large shallot or ¼ red onion

½ large cored Asian pear

½ cup loosely packed basil leaves

½ cup loosely packed cilantro leaves, stems removed

VINAIGRETTE

2 Tbsp white or rice vinegar

1 Tbsp fish sauce

1 Tbsp sugar

2 Tbsp avocado, canola or safflower oil

Trim the stalk off the fennel and cut the bulb in half vertically. Remove the core of the fennel by cutting it out at the base in a V-shape. Using a mandoline or sharp knife, slice the fennel about ⅛ inch thick. It should be thick enough to hold its shape but thin enough to resemble a slaw with a good crunch to it. Place into a medium-sized bowl. Repeat the same process with the cabbage and shallot.

Slice the Asian pear into very thin wedges and add those to the bowl. Chill the sliced veg and fruit in the fridge until serving.

To make the vinaigrette, in a small bowl, whisk together the vinegar, fish sauce and sugar until the sugar has dissolved. Whisk in the oil, stirring continuously.

Right before serving, toss the vinaigrette with the slaw, basil and cilantro leaves.

MAKE AHEAD

Slice the fennel, cabbage and shallot the morning of, and keep in an ice bath in the fridge. Drain and pat dry before serving.

CHOPPED MIDDLE EASTERN SALAD WITH HUMMUS DRESSING

SERVES 4–6

I love a chopped salad any way it comes. Polo Bar style with bacon and blue cheese, Palm Beach style with hearts of palm and avocado, even airport style with iceberg, chickpeas and canned olives. I'll take them all. This chopped salad uses similar ingredients as a fattoush, with the addition of quick-pickled onions and a hummus and cumin dressing. It's herb-forward, with basil, mint and dill practically replacing the need for lettuce. I lightly pickle the red onions in this recipe because I like how it mellows the bite and keeps them crispy.

SALAD

½ cup apple cider vinegar

1 tsp kosher salt

1 Tbsp granulated sugar

¼ red onion, thinly sliced into rounds

2 cups grape tomatoes, halved

½ English cucumber, quartered lengthwise and cut in ½-inch pieces

One 19 oz can chickpeas, drained and rinsed

1 cup tightly packed basil leaves

½ cup tightly packed mint leaves

¼ cup tightly packed dill

½ cup crumbled sheep's milk feta

HUMMUS DRESSING

3 Tbsp hummus

½ tsp cumin

2 Tbsp lemon juice

½ tsp kosher salt

Black pepper, to taste

2 Tbsp olive oil

In a small bowl, whisk together the vinegar, salt and sugar until dissolved. Add the sliced onions and press down to submerge in the vinegar. Remove the onions after 15 minutes and discard the liquid.

Place the onions, tomatoes, cucumbers and chickpeas in a large serving bowl.

For the dressing, in a small bowl, whisk together the hummus, cumin, lemon juice, salt, pepper and olive oil until smooth and pourable.

Gather all the herbs together in a large pile and run your knife over them four to five times, very roughly chopping them before adding them to the salad. Toss with the dressing and top with the feta. Serve with some grilled chicken and pitas on the side, if you like.

ROASTED POTATO SALAD WITH GHERKINS & DILL

SERVES 4–6

Potatoes, gherkins and dill get along like a house on fire. Instead of boiling, I'm roasting the potatoes, and instead of a mayo dressing, I've opted for a grainy mustard vinaigrette. Throwing in a few handfuls of arugula lightens this up and makes it a well-rounded side that goes particularly well with the Salt & Pepper Flank Steak with Quick Tomato Shallot Kimchi on p. 195. If you can't find fingerling potatoes, baby potatoes work perfectly well.

SALAD

1 lb (about 12–15) fingerling potatoes, halved lengthwise

2 Tbsp olive oil

½ tsp kosher salt

Black pepper, to taste

4 cups arugula

10–12 gherkins, thinly sliced into rounds

½ cup loosely packed dill fronds

GRAINY MUSTARD VINAIGRETTE

1 Tbsp grainy Dijon mustard

2 Tbsp minced dill

½ tsp grated garlic

1 tsp kosher salt

Black pepper, to taste

2 Tbsp apple cider vinegar

3 Tbsp olive oil

Preheat the oven to 400°F and line a baking sheet with parchment paper.

Place the potatoes on the lined baking sheet and toss with the olive oil, salt and pepper. Roast, cut side down, for 25–30 minutes, until golden brown, slightly crispy and cooked through. Remove from heat and allow to cool slightly while making the vinaigrette.

In a small bowl, whisk together the Dijon, dill, garlic, salt, pepper and vinegar. Drizzle in the olive oil and continue whisking until combined.

Place the arugula in a large shallow bowl. Top with the warm potatoes and gherkin slices. Toss with the vinaigrette and dill fronds to finish.

MAKE AHEAD

Roast the potatoes up to 1 day ahead and allow to come to room temperature before serving. The vinaigrette can be made 3 days in advance.

SLICED TOMATOES WITH PROSCIUTTO & PARM-ARUGULA SALT

SERVES 4

4 ripe heirloom or beefsteak tomatoes

8 slices good-quality prosciutto

3 Tbsp olive oil + more for drizzling

2 Tbsp lemon juice, divided

2 cups packed arugula

½ cup finely grated Parmigiano-Reggiano

½ tsp kosher salt

1 tsp black pepper

What is Parm-arugula salt, you ask? A clever name for a salty, flavorful sprinkle that you'll throw on tomatoes (and likely a lot more once you've tried it). It's a great way to use up some arugula that might be past its prime. Use big, juicy tomatoes in the summer or cherry tomatoes in the winter. (Also, anytime I can "casually drape" prosciutto over a peak summer tomato is a good eating day for me.)

Slice the tomatoes into ½-inch slices and lay on a platter. Casually drape the prosciutto over the tomatoes and drizzle with 3 tablespoons of the olive oil and 1 tablespoon of the lemon juice.

Mince the arugula leaves until very fine. Toss in a small bowl with the grated Parm, salt and pepper. Make sure you do this at the last minute, as the Parm will start to absorb the moisture from the arugula. Liberally sprinkle over the tomatoes and prosciutto. Drizzle with a little more olive oil and the remaining 1 tablespoon of lemon juice, and serve immediately.

RECOVERY SOUP

SERVES 4

2 leeks, white and light green parts only

2 Tbsp olive oil

6 cloves garlic, very thinly sliced

1 Tbsp grated fresh ginger

6 cups good-quality chicken or beef bone stock

1 bunch Swiss chard

2 cups cooked quinoa

One 19 oz can chickpeas, drained and rinsed

1 tsp lemon zest

Kosher salt and black pepper, to taste

I have to say that I get very possessive about this soup. I make a big batch and keep it in an unmarked container in the fridge for impromptu lunches or even when a 4 p.m. hunger pang kicks in. It's an excellent soup for when you're fighting a cold or have had a rough week or a late night. It's filling and satisfying and deeply nutritious.

Slice the leeks into ¼-inch thick rounds and put them in a large bowl with cold water. Agitate the water and leeks with your hands to remove any sand or dirt, which will sink to the bottom of the bowl. Remove the leeks and pat them dry on paper towels.

In a large pot over medium-high heat, heat the oil. Add the leeks, garlic and ginger and sauté for 3–4 minutes, until the leeks are soft and translucent.

Add the stock and bring to a low boil.

Clean and trim the Swiss chard into 2-inch pieces. Add to the stock along with the cooked quinoa, chickpeas and lemon zest. Taste for seasoning—certain stocks are saltier than others, so I'll leave this up to you. Let the chard wilt for a few minutes, then serve.

SWEET POTATO, LENTIL & COCONUT MILK SOUP

SERVES 6

1 Tbsp coconut oil

1 medium yellow onion, diced

2 cloves garlic, crushed and roughly chopped

1 tsp grated fresh ginger

½ tsp cumin

3 tsp curry powder

¼ tsp cinnamon

1 tsp kosher salt + more to taste

Black pepper, to taste

2 large sweet potatoes, peeled and chopped in 1-inch chunks

¾ cup dried red lentils

½ cup roughly chopped jarred roasted red peppers

4 cups chicken or vegetable stock

One 14 fl oz can full-fat coconut milk

Juice of 1 lime + wedges for serving

Coconut yogurt, for serving (optional)

This soup speaks to me. It's "health giving," as Nigella would say, and deeply satisfying. A curry without being a curry, a soup without being a soup, it hovers somewhere between the two. Serve it over some brown rice for extra heft or on its own with a salad. Kids love it. Adults love it. You'll love it.

In a large pot over medium heat, heat the coconut oil until melted. Add the onions, garlic and ginger and sauté until the onions are transparent and fragrant, about 2 minutes.

Add the cumin, curry powder, cinnamon, salt and pepper and sauté for 1 more minute. Add the sweet potatoes, lentils and peppers to the pot and top with the chicken stock and coconut milk. All the vegetables should be submerged in the liquid.

Bring to a simmer and place a lid on the pot, allowing a little space for steam to escape. Simmer for 30 minutes, until the potatoes are very tender and the lentils are cooked.

Remove from the heat and mash three or four times with a potato masher. You still want a lot of texture, but you want to break up any large chunks of potatoes. Taste and adjust the seasoning with more salt and pepper. Stir in the lime juice and serve with lime wedges. I love serving this with a spoonful of coconut yogurt on top.

CELERY ROOT SOUP WITH SOURDOUGH CROUTONS & BACON

SERVES 6

4 Tbsp olive oil, divided, + more for drizzling

8 slices bacon, sliced in ½-inch pieces

1 yellow onion, roughly chopped

2 cloves garlic, crushed and roughly chopped

5 stalks celery, chopped in ½-inch pieces

One 1 lb celery root, peeled and chopped in 1-inch pieces

2 tsp kosher salt + more to taste, and for croutons

Black pepper, to taste

4 cups chicken stock

Two 1-inch-thick slices sourdough bread

Juice of 1 lemon

I feel like celery root soup sort of had its moment in the sun. It was a soup that you would often spot in the aughts at fancy-lunch restaurants, maybe with some truffle oil involved, or maybe something like crème fraîche. Not necessarily something that would always be recreated with the best success at home. Well, here in the 2020s, I've ditched any remnants of cream or butter and lightened it up with olive oil and stock. Bacon and sourdough bring some texture and smokiness and generally make this a more delicious soup.

Preheat the oven to 400°F and line a baking sheet with parchment paper.

In a large stockpot over medium-high heat, heat 2 tablespoons olive oil. Add the bacon and cook until crispy. Remove with a slotted spoon and drain the bacon on paper towels.

Add the onions and garlic to the bacon fat in the pot and cook for 2–3 minutes, until softened. Add the celery, celery root, salt, pepper and chicken stock. Bring the stock to a simmer and cover with a lid. Simmer for 30 minutes, until the celery and celery root are very tender.

While the soup is simmering, cut the sourdough into ½-inch cubes. Toss on the parchment-lined baking sheet with the remaining 2 tablespoons olive oil and some salt and pepper. Bake for 10 minutes before tossing and checking for doneness. The croutons should be golden brown and crispy, with a little softness still remaining in the center.

Remove the soup from the heat and carefully transfer it to a blender using a ladle. Blend until smooth. Stir in the lemon juice and season to taste with salt and pepper.

Serve in bowls with the croutons and bacon scattered overtop. Drizzle with a little extra olive oil, if you like.

VEGETABLES

VEGETABLES HAVE DEFINITELY ARRIVED.

We're experimenting more with vegetables, we're treating them like full meals, we're making them the star of the table. Showstopping vegetable dishes that get the same "ooohs" and "ahhhs" that the rack of lamb hitting the table once did—this is a very good thing.

So many chefs have influenced the way I cook and present vegetables, but in the end, my methodology comes down to good-quality ingredients and taking advantage of them when they are at their peak. Spring onions and asparagus after the snow has melted. Summer tomatoes and corn that will make you sing. Roasting, grilling, charring and coaxing the flavors out of root vegetables, winter squash and eggplant. It doesn't take much to make a vegetable shine. A pile of fresh herbs, a sprinkle of salt, a hit of a crunchy seed or nut. It's not complicated.

Some of these dishes are looking for a protein main to saddle up to, while others would hold their own as the main event themselves. Dinner party–friendly and easy to pull off (as is the goal with everything here, let's be honest), this is a collection of veg that you'll be able to revisit throughout the year because, after all, for every season there is a vegetable, and for every vegetable there is someone hungry to enjoy it.

ROASTED ACORN SQUASH WITH HAZELNUT & FRIED ROSEMARY

SERVES 4–6

2 medium acorn squash, skin washed well

¼ cup + 2 Tbsp olive oil, divided

2 Tbsp balsamic vinegar

½ tsp kosher salt

Black pepper, to taste

½ cup hazelnuts

1 Tbsp packed fresh rosemary leaves

Juice of ½ lemon

I really like vegetables that I don't have to peel. The thin skin of the acorn squash becomes tender with roasting, and balsamic vinegar aids in its caramelization. If you're not roasting essentially all of your veg with a little hit of vinegar, you are missing out. It's the secret ingredient I use in roasting everything from potatoes to tomatoes and Brussels sprouts. Frying the rosemary at the last minute and pouring the crispy herbs and infused oil over the squash add such a great layer and depth of earthy flavor. You could really use any toasted nut or seed here, like walnuts, pepitas or pecans. Personally, I like the richness from hazelnuts, especially paired with rosemary. Serve this one warm or at room temperature. And I'll just say that this dish loves the Thanksgiving table.

Preheat your oven to 375°F and line a baking sheet with parchment paper.

Cut the squash into ½-inch rings, leaving the skin on. Remove and discard the seeds. In slightly overlapping layers (you might not fit all in an even layer, which is okay), place the squash rings on the lined baking sheet. Drizzle with ¼ cup olive oil and the balsamic vinegar, then sprinkle with the salt and pepper. Roast the squash for 30–35 minutes on a lower rack in the oven, flipping once halfway through. The squash should be light golden, caramelized around the edges and fork-tender. The skin is totally edible at this point. Transfer the roasted squash to a large platter.

Meanwhile, as the squash roasts, place the hazelnuts on a separate baking sheet and toast on the upper rack of the oven for 5–8 minutes in the oven, until the skins are deep brown. Remove from the oven and place on a clean dishcloth. Pull the corners of the cloth up and around the nuts and rub to remove the papery skins. Roughly chop the hazelnuts and scatter over the squash.

Heat a small pan over high heat. Add the remaining 2 tablespoons olive oil and the rosemary leaves. Fry for 15–20 seconds, or until the leaves become fragrant and take on a light golden color. Spoon the rosemary leaves and oil over the squash and sprinkle with lemon juice. Serve warm or at room temperature.

MAKE AHEAD
Toast and skin the hazelnuts up to 1 week beforehand and keep in the fridge.

HASSELBACK SQUASH WITH CUMIN YOGURT & POMEGRANATE

SERVES 4

1 large butternut squash (see note)

1 Tbsp + ¼ cup olive oil, divided

¾ tsp kosher salt, divided

Black pepper, to taste

1 tsp grated garlic

½ cup plain Greek yogurt

¼ tsp cinnamon

½ tsp cumin

½ cup pomegranate seeds

½ cup cilantro leaves
and tender stems, left whole

I adore a hearty vegetable that can hold its weight next to any platter of meat. This carvable, shareable dish can be the star of a vegetarian dinner or a side for any meat lover. It's versatile as a side or a main—it doesn't care, it just wants you to be happy. Hasselbacking any firm veg is a prime way to increase crispiness and flavor. Think about all those edges being kissed by the heat of the oven and all those crannies begging to soak up more cumin-scented yogurt.

Preheat the oven to 425°F and line a baking sheet with parchment paper.

Using a vegetable peeler, remove the skin of the butternut squash. Carefully halve the squash lengthwise and scoop out the seeds. Coat the squash halves with 1 tablespoon olive oil and season with ½ teaspoon salt and pepper. Roast for 15 minutes flat side down on the lined baking sheet until slightly tender but still firm. Carefully transfer the squash to a cutting board, being careful not to break it.

In a small bowl, mix the remaining ¼ cup olive oil with the grated garlic and stir well to combine.

Once the squash is cool enough to touch, use a sharp knife to gently score the back of the squash, with each cut going about ½ inch deep and ¼ inch apart, being careful not to cut all the way through. Brush the squash with the garlic oil and place back into the oven until the squash is tender and golden, about 30 minutes.

Mix the yogurt with the cinnamon, cumin, remaining ¼ teaspoon salt and pepper. Add a couple of tablespoons of water to reach the desirable drizzle consistency.

Transfer the squash to a platter, spoon on the yogurt and sprinkle with pomegranate seeds and cilantro.

NOTE
Par-baking the squash allows for easy cutting. When hasselbacking, be careful not to cut more than about halfway through. If you go too far and slice the squash in half, just stick it back together. No one will know, especially when it's drizzled with the yogurt, pomegranate and cilantro.

MAKE AHEAD
Peel and par-bake the squash up to the day before. Refrigerate on the baking tray, covered with plastic wrap, until ready to cook.

CARAMELIZED CABBAGE WITH PEANUTS, GREEN ONION & SOY GLAZE

SERVES 4

1 green cabbage, cut in 8 wedges

¼ cup coconut oil, melted

2 Tbsp maple syrup

3 Tbsp soy sauce

1 tsp chili flakes

Kosher salt and black pepper, to taste

3 green onions, white and light green parts only, minced

⅓ cup salted peanuts, roughly chopped

Juice of 1–2 limes

Sambal oelek or sriracha, for drizzling

The texture of roasted and caramelized cabbage is heavenly. It's like roasted Brussels sprouts but infinitely better. More tender, sweeter and less, shall we say, cruciferous? This is one underrated vegetable and it can swing with all flavor profiles. I've done this method before with pancetta and red onions on the Crumb website, and that's also wonderful. Serve this beauty alongside the Miso Sesame Chicken on p. 180 or with the Stir-Fried Pork with Pineapple & Green Onion on p. 199.

Preheat the oven to 425°F and line a baking sheet with parchment paper. Place the cabbage wedges on the baking sheet on their sides.

In a large bowl, whisk together the coconut oil, maple syrup, soy sauce, chili flakes, salt and pepper. Brush liberally over both sides of the cabbage.

Bake for approximately 45 minutes, flipping once until soft and caramelized around the outer leaves. Liquid will drain from the cabbage into the pan, which is normal.

Remove from the oven and transfer to a serving platter. Sprinkle the green onions and crushed peanuts overtop, followed by the lime juice (only use 1 lime if they're especially juicy) and hot sauce to taste.

MASHED SWEET POTATOES WITH COCONUT MILK & TURMERIC

SERVES 4–6

3 large sweet potatoes

1 cup full-fat coconut milk + more if needed and for finishing

1 tsp turmeric + a sprinkle for finishing

½ tsp cinnamon

1 tsp grated fresh ginger

1 tsp kosher salt

This is one of my favorite winter sides to serve with just about anything. It's comfort food that feels nourishing and cozy but has some interest and depth from the ginger, turmeric and cinnamon. As sweet potatoes are quite a lot wetter than regular potatoes, the amount of liquid needed is far less than a traditional mash. If you have a ricer, use it to mash the potatoes. I prefer this tool, as it makes them the smoothest, but if you don't have one, use a traditional masher to make the potatoes as smooth as possible. I omit using any oil or butter, but a dollop of ghee in here would not go amiss. Infusing the coconut milk with the spices gives them that little boost to really shine through. I like drizzling the finished dish with a few spoons of coconut milk—it looks so pretty like this.

Bring a large pot of salted water to a boil. Peel and cube the potatoes into 1-inch chunks. Boil for 15 minutes, or until very tender and cooked through. Drain and return to the pot. Mash, and stir over a low heat for 1 minute to remove any excess moisture.

In a small saucepan, heat the coconut milk with the turmeric, cinnamon and ginger until simmering. Add the infused coconut milk and the salt to the potatoes and stir until the milk is absorbed. Add more coconut milk if it's too thick.

Serve in a bowl, creating a swoop with the back of a spoon. Drizzle in a little more coconut milk and a sprinkling of turmeric.

MAKE AHEAD
Boil your potatoes the day before and keep them in a ziplock bag until ready to mash.

SMOKY FRIED CORN & ZUCCHINI WITH BACON & LIME

SERVES 4-6

2–3 Tbsp olive oil, divided

6 slices bacon, cut in 2-inch chunks

2 small or 1 large zucchini, sliced in ¼-inch rounds

8 ears corn, kernels removed

1 tsp grated garlic

1 tsp smoked paprika

1 tsp kosher salt

Black pepper, to taste

1 cup packed basil leaves, roughly torn

1 cup packed cilantro leaves and tender stems, left whole

Zest and juice of 1 lime + wedges for serving

1 cup grape tomatoes, halved

½ cup crumbled sheep's milk feta

Until my kids have got their adult teeth fully in, we'll be eating corn off the cob for a while. Lucky us, because this recipe beats any corn on the cob I've had. This is an update of a favorite simple side my mom would make when we were kids. I added the bacon (because corn loves bacon like I love bacon), removed the white pepper (in my honest opinion, white pepper has no place in my kitchen) and fried the coins of zucchini until golden and sweet. It's important that the zucchini and corn come to room temperature before assembly so they don't wilt all the lovely fresh herbs. This would be so tasty with the Butterflied Grilled Shrimp with Charred Green Onion Yogurt Sauce on p. 166.

In a large skillet over medium-high heat, heat 1 tablespoon oil. Add the bacon and cook until crispy. Remove the bacon with a slotted spoon and drain on paper towels. Wipe any extra fat out of the pan.

Reheat the pan over high heat, add 1 tablespoon olive oil and place the zucchini in one layer, trying not to overlap the slices. You will have to do this in batches. Allow the zucchini to brown for 2–3 minutes before flipping and browning the other side, then transfer to a large plate. Repeat with the remaining zucchini, adding more olive oil to the pan if needed. Once the pan is empty, add the corn and the garlic, along with the paprika, salt and pepper. Sauté the corn for 2–3 minutes, until just cooked. Transfer the corn to the plate with the zucchini and allow to cool for at least 10 minutes.

Place the corn, zucchini, bacon, basil, cilantro, lime zest and tomatoes in a shallow bowl and toss well. Drizzle with lime juice and top with feta. Garnish with more lime wedges.

A PILE OF ROOT VEG OVER GREEN TAHINI

SERVES 4–6

Here's an entertainer's dream: an herbaceous swoosh of tahini piled high with roasted root vegetables. Dramatic! Impressive! Easy? Now there's the reality. The best part of this dreamy scenario may just be how easy it is to pull off. You can cook it all in advance, leave it at room temp and then just warm it up in the oven before serving. It's what dinner parties and fall/winter entertaining should be made of.

4 carrots, peeled and halved lengthwise

1 small sweet potato, peeled and cut in 1-inch cubes

6–8 large Brussels sprouts, halved lengthwise

4 parsnips, peeled and quartered lengthwise

1 small acorn squash, skin on, seeds removed, sliced in ¼-inch rings

⅓ cup olive oil

1 tsp kosher salt

Black pepper, to taste

2 Tbsp balsamic vinegar

Juice of 1 lemon, for serving

GREEN TAHINI

¾ cup tahini

1 clove garlic, roughly chopped

1 tsp kosher salt

Juice of 1 lemon

½ cup packed flat-leaf parsley leaves

½ cup packed dill fronds

Preheat the oven to 425°F and line two baking sheets with parchment paper.

Place the veggies in one layer on the lined baking sheets, and toss together with the olive oil, salt, pepper and balsamic vinegar. Roast for 20–25 minutes, or until the veggies are tender and starting to brown.

While the veggies are roasting, place the tahini, garlic, salt, lemon juice, parsley, dill and ¼ cup cold water in a high-speed blender. Blend until very smooth.

Spoon the green tahini into the middle of a platter, pile the root vegetables overtop and squeeze with lemon.

SQUASH RINGS WITH YOGURT RANCH

SERVES 4–6

2 delicata squash

2 Tbsp olive oil

1 tsp kosher salt, divided

Black pepper, to taste

½ cup plain Greek yogurt (at least 2% fat)

¼ cup whole or 2% milk

2 tsp minced dill

2 tsp minced chives

½ tsp grated garlic

Juice of 1 lemon

This one is fun. Squash rings—fun?? But hear me out. A quick roasting will turn your basic winter squash into a sweet caramelized treat, worthy of your favorite local restaurant's seasonal veg menu, but the kicker is the yogurt ranch sauce that you're about to dip them in (aka *THE* homemade ranch sauce that you're about to dip everything in). Delicata squash can sometimes be tricky to find. A small butternut squash is your next-best bet.

Preheat the oven to 425°F and line two baking sheets with parchment paper.

Slice the squash into ½-inch rounds, keeping the seeds intact (see note), and toss in a bowl with the olive oil, ½ teaspoon salt and pepper. Lay in a single layer on the lined baking sheets. Bake for 18–20 minutes, until tender and starting to brown around the edges.

In a medium-sized bowl, whisk together the yogurt, milk, dill, chives, garlic, lemon juice, the remaining ½ teaspoon salt and pepper until well combined. Taste for seasoning and adjust if needed.

Pile the squash rings on a platter and serve the ranch dipping sauce on the side.

NOTE
I don't bother removing the seeds, as I like it when they get crispy from roasting—just like pumpkin seeds.

CRISPY EGGPLANT WITH VINEGARED TOMATOES & GARLIC

SERVES 4

½ cup + 2 Tbsp olive oil, divided

2 large eggplants, cut in 1-inch slices

2 cups grape tomatoes, halved

⅓ cup red wine vinegar

1 tsp grated garlic

1 shallot, sliced very thinly in rings

1 tsp kosher salt

Black pepper, to taste

½ cup packed flat-leaf parsley leaves, torn

½ cup packed basil leaves, torn

I love this simple cooking method for eggplant because it gets dark brown and sort of crispy. Make sure to cut thick slices, as the eggplant collapses when it cooks and needs some heft to hold together. The eggplant slices will soak up the vinegary juices from the tomatoes like sponges. It looks like a lot of vinegar, but just trust. Paired with the Sheet-Pan Salmon with Chickpeas & Basil-Olive Salsa (p. 163), this really is the perfect meal.

Preheat the oven to 400°F and line a baking sheet with parchment paper.

Pour ½ cup of olive oil into a shallow bowl. Dip the eggplant slices in the oil, coating both sides.

Bake for 35 minutes on the lined baking sheet, flipping once halfway through cooking.

In a medium-sized bowl, toss the tomatoes, vinegar, garlic and shallots with the remaining 2 tablespoons of oil and the salt and pepper. Let the tomatoes marinate while the eggplant is cooking.

Place the eggplant on a large serving dish, spooning the tomatoes and their liquid overtop, then finish with the torn parsley and basil leaves. Serve warm or at room temperature.

CACIO E PEPE
CRISPY POTATO CAKE

SERVES 4

4–5 large Yukon Gold potatoes

¼ cup melted unsalted butter, divided

1½ tsp kosher salt, divided

1 tsp black pepper, divided

1 cup finely grated pecorino romano or
Parmigiano-Reggiano, divided

Never have potatoes done their job so well. If you like a latke, if you love rosti, you will totally be into a crispy potato cake. Inspired by Nigel Slater and his deliciously layered spuds, this one looks fancy but is dead simple. This lands in my kids' top five favorite dishes—and with so many crispy bits and delicious morsels, I'm totally with them.

Preheat the oven to 375°F.

Wash the skin of the potatoes. Using a mandoline, slice the potatoes into very thin rounds.

Pour 1 tablespoon of melted butter into the bottom of a 9-inch cast-iron frying pan. Concentrically layer one-third of the potatoes around the bottom of the pan. Drizzle with another tablespoon of butter, ½ teaspoon salt, one-third of the pepper and ⅓ cup pecorino. Repeat this process two more times, but reserve the last ⅓ cup of pecorino for later.

Bake for 45–50 minutes. The potatoes should be knife-tender and dark golden brown around the edges. Sprinkle with the remaining ⅓ cup cheese, then bake for another 5 minutes. Serve large wedges straight from the pan.

SLOW-ROASTED BABY POTATOES WITH ROMESCO DIPPING SAUCE

SERVES 4

1 lb baby potatoes

1 Tbsp baking soda

1 cup blanched (skinless) almonds

3 Tbsp + ½ cup olive oil, divided

1½ tsp kosher salt, divided

Black pepper, to taste

1 medium clove garlic, roughly chopped

½ tsp smoked paprika

1 cup jarred roasted red peppers, drained

2 tsp white or red wine vinegar

Think of this one as grown-up hash browns with ketchup. Except instead of frying, we're roasting (which makes for an extra-crispy exterior and super-soft interior), and instead of ketchup, we're dipping into a rich and robust romesco sauce. Romesco is traditionally made with almonds, as I've done here, but you could try it with walnuts too. This recipe makes just under two cups of romesco, so save it for serving with veggies, fish or chicken. And if you're pinched for time, you can skip the baking-soda soak for the potatoes, though I find it makes the interior creamier.

Preheat the oven to 400°F. Line two baking sheets with parchment paper.

Cut the potatoes in half and submerge in a large bowl of cold water along with the baking soda. Allow to soak for 1–3 hours. This helps remove some of the starch from the potatoes, which results in potatoes that are crispy on the outside and creamy on the inside.

Place the blanched almonds on one baking sheet and bake for 4–5 minutes, until golden. Watch closely to make sure they don't burn. Remove and set aside to cool.

Remove the potatoes from the water and pat dry. Toss in a bowl with 3 tablespoons of olive oil, 1 teaspoon of kosher salt and pepper to taste. Place the potatoes cut side down on the second baking sheet. Bake for 30 minutes, until golden brown.

While the potatoes are baking, make the romesco. Place the remaining ½ cup olive oil, ½ teaspoon of kosher salt, pepper, almonds, garlic, paprika, red peppers and vinegar in a food processor or high-speed blender. Blend until a chunky paste forms. Season with more salt and pepper to taste.

Spoon the romesco onto a platter and use the back of a spoon to spread it over the plate in a large swoosh. Scatter the warm potatoes overtop.

MAKE AHEAD

Soak your potatoes the morning of, pat dry and **wrap in** a clean dishcloth until ready to bake. You can make **the rome**sco 2 days in advance.

PAN-SEARED SUGAR SNAPS & RADISH WITH MISO DRESSING

SERVES 4–6

4–5 small to medium radishes

1 Tbsp grapeseed or safflower oil

1 lb sugar snap peas, strings removed

1 tsp lemon zest

1 Tbsp finely chopped chives

Black pepper

MISO DRESSING

1 Tbsp white miso paste

2 Tbsp lime juice

¼ tsp kosher salt

1 Tbsp honey or maple syrup

1 Tbsp grapeseed, avocado or safflower oil

1 tsp toasted sesame oil

This side comes together in a cool five minutes. The sugar snaps turn a vivid green when kissed by the heat of the pan, and the pink edges of the crisp radishes make this one of the prettiest recipes in the book. I love the miso dressing that gets tossed into the pan—it flavors the crisp beans and radishes much better than a pinch of salt and pepper ever could. In fact, I love using miso paste to season in a similar way I would use soy sauce. It's got the umami factor that adds an extra layer of flavor without any extra effort on your part.

Using a mandoline or sharp knife, slice the radishes as thin as possible. Place the slices in a bowl of ice water. This makes the radishes impossibly crisp and slightly curled at the edges.

To make the miso dressing, in a small bowl, whisk together the miso paste with the lime juice and salt. Add the honey and both oils and whisk until combined.

In a large frying pan over high heat, heat the grapeseed oil for 1 minute. Add the sugar snap peas and sauté for 2 minutes, or until bright green but still crunchy. Add the dressing and the lemon zest to the pan and toss with the sugar snap peas for 30 seconds.

Remove the sugar snap peas from the heat, drain the radishes and transfer the two to a large platter. Toss to coat in the dressing, and sprinkle the chives and some black pepper overtop.

TRAY-BAKE BROCCOLI WITH BROKEN BEANS, LEMON & GARLIC

SERVES 4

1 large or 2 small heads broccoli

One 14 oz can cannellini beans, drained and rinsed

1 lemon, skin washed well

⅓ cup olive oil

1 tsp grated garlic

1 tsp kosher salt

Black pepper, to taste

A complete side all in one. My favorite way to eat and cook broccoli is roasted. It maintains a delicious crunch but takes on a deeper flavor, especially when it has little bits of char around the edges. And what are broken beans? When you roast canned cannellini beans, the skin crackles and they fall apart slightly, but the interior takes on a creamy texture that is rich and delicious. This bakes all on one tray at the same time and is delicious with the Leg of Lamb with Hot Honey, Feta & Olives on p. 191.

Preheat the oven to 375°F and line a baking sheet with parchment paper.

Peel the stalk of the broccoli with a vegetable peeler, removing the tough outer skin. Cut the broccoli crown into florets and the stalk into ¼-inch coins. Place the broccoli on the tray along with the drained and rinsed beans.

Slice eight paper-thin slices of lemon and reserve the remainder for the juice. Place the slices of lemon on the tray with the broccoli and beans.

In a small bowl, mix together the olive oil and garlic. Pour the garlic oil over the vegetables, and sprinkle with the salt and pepper. Use your hands to toss well.

Bake for 25–30 minutes, until the broccoli is charred around the edges and the beans take on a light golden color. Finish with a squeeze of lemon juice.

ROASTED CAULIFLOWER & POTATOES WITH TURMERIC

SERVES 4

1 lb baby potatoes, halved

1 medium head cauliflower, cut into florets

3 medium shallots, peeled and quartered

1 Tbsp grated ginger

⅓ cup melted coconut oil

1 tsp kosher salt

1 tsp turmeric

½ tsp cumin

Black pepper, to taste

1 tsp honey

1½ tsp red wine vinegar

Flat-leaf parsley, for garnish

This recipe is inspired by my love of aloo gobi, a traditional Indian cauliflower and potato dish using spices and aromatics to create warmth and depth. This is all baked at the same time on a sheet pan for a simple cleanup. I drizzle the finished roasted veggies with a tiny bit of honey and vinegar, which adds a whole other dimension of flavor. Similar to how Indian food loves chutney, this sweet, vinegary hit allows the dish to shine.

Preheat the oven to 375°F and line a baking sheet with parchment paper.

Put the cut baby potatoes, cauliflower and shallots on the lined baking sheet. Mix the grated ginger into the coconut oil and drizzle over the veggies, followed by the salt, turmeric, cumin and black pepper. Toss with your hands until well coated.

Bake for 35–40 minutes, until the cauliflower is beginning to brown and the potatoes are tender. Transfer the veggies to a platter. Drizzle with honey and vinegar and toss again. Garnish with fresh parsley leaves.

SUMMER RATATOUILLE WITH TAHINI VINAIGRETTE

SERVES 6

2 medium zucchini,
sliced on the bias ½ inch thick

½ red onion, sliced in ¼-inch rounds
and separated into rings

2 Tbsp olive oil

½ tsp kosher salt + more to taste

Black pepper, to taste

2–3 large heirloom tomatoes,
sliced ¼-inch thick

1 cup yellow grape tomatoes, halved

TAHINI VINAIGRETTE

⅓ cup tahini

½ tsp grated garlic

½ tsp kosher salt

¼ tsp chili flakes

Juice of 1 lemon

⅓ cup olive oil

This is likely a recipe you will make once and then keep coming back to over and over again. For one, the presentation is a showstopper, and the simple nature of the ingredients makes this an easy recipe, using little time and effort. I also love the raw tomatoes with the slightly warm grilled zucchini and onions. It's a play of texture and temperature that is just delicious. The tahini vinaigrette pulls this whole dish together to make it sing. The recipe for the tahini vinaigrette will give you more than you need, but you can keep it for any salads the week brings your way. It's delicious on just about any leafy green.

In a medium bowl, toss the zucchini and onion rings with the olive oil, salt and pepper. Grill the vegetables for 2–3 minutes per side, until slightly charred and tender. Remove and set aside until they come to room temperature. You can also pan-fry the zucchini and onions using the same timing.

To make the vinaigrette, in a medium bowl, whisk together the tahini, garlic, salt, chili flakes, lemon juice and olive oil. The mixture will begin to seize up and become very thick and sticky. Spoon in 4–6 tablespoons of water and stir well. Add more water for a thinner consistency. It should resemble a very thick cream.

Lay the tomato slices on a platter. Place the zucchini in between the tomatoes. Scatter with the onions and grape tomatoes.

Drizzle about ½ cup of tahini vinaigrette over the vegetables and season with a little extra salt and pepper. Store any extra vinaigrette in an airtight container in the fridge for up to 1 week.

MAKE AHEAD

Grill the zucchini and onions up to 2 hours in advance and keep at room temperature. You can make the vinaigrette up to 1 week in advance.

BAKED ONION RINGS WITH DINER DIPPING SAUCE

SERVES 4

ONION RINGS

2 large Vidalia onions

1 cup all-purpose flour

1 tsp kosher salt + more for baking

1 scant cup 2% milk

2 Tbsp white vinegar

1 box panko bread crumbs

2 Tbsp vegetable oil, for drizzling

DINER SAUCE

1 cup mayonnaise

2 Tbsp minced dill pickles

1 Tbsp ketchup

4 dashes Worcestershire sauce

½ tsp grated garlic

Black pepper, to taste

I know what you're thinking. How can BAKED onion rings be as good or as crispy as fried onion rings? Well, I am here to tell you that they are the disruptor of the onion-ring world. Not only are they crispy beyond belief, they are an easy weekday side to pull off, as there's no big pot of hot oil and deep-frying involved. The trick is a quick buttermilk batter made by mixing milk and vinegar and then relying on a coating of panko for the super-shaggy crunch. The sauce here is, let's be honest, a dead ringer for Big Mac sauce, so it's fast-food vibes in a slow-food kind of way.

Preheat the oven to 375°F and line two baking sheets with parchment paper.

Peel the onions and cut them into ¾-inch slices. Separate the onion rings, discarding the very small inner rings.

Place the flour and salt in a medium-sized bowl. Measure out 1 scant cup of milk and add the 2 tablespoons of vinegar to the measuring cup. The milk will immediately begin to curdle, which is what we want here. Let sit for 2 minutes, then pour the milk mixture into the flour and whisk with a fork until smooth.

Divide the panko between two separate shallow bowls. The reason for this is that the batter on the onion rings starts to make the panko clumpy after a few dips, so it's good to keep a fresh bowl of panko for when this happens.

Dip the onions one by one into the batter, letting any excess batter drip back into the bowl. Press the onion rings into the panko and flip to coat on the other side. Gather up some crumbs and sprinkle on top to make sure they are coated very well. Once the first bowl of panko starts to get lumpy from the batter, start with the fresh bowl. Place the dredged onion rings on the baking sheet about ½ inch apart to allow for maximum crispiness.

Use a spoon to drizzle a little oil on each onion ring and sprinkle with more salt. Bake for 25–30 minutes, until light golden brown.

While the onion rings are baking, mix together all the ingredients for the diner sauce.

Serve the onion rings immediately with diner sauce on the side and marvel at the crunch.

MAKE AHEAD

You can make the diner sauce up to 1 day in advance and keep it in the fridge. Bring to room temperature when ready to serve.

WEEKEND
ADVENTURES

AHH, THE WEEKEND.

Slower pace, more friends, less fuss. The weekend is when we bake, it's when we sleep in and when we brunch and then continue to eat at all hours of the day. The weekend is a reset.

Sure, the concept of a "weekend" may have changed during the last year or so, as I wrote this book and as our daily routines were uprooted, but all the more reason to celebrate time at home with food and the ones we love—even if the ones we love are also the ones we get annoyed with.

From savory eggy dishes (after all, what is a weekend without eggs?) to sweets that just barely pass as breakfast, I've included the meals that my own family continues to enjoy week after week. Old world (my Belgian grandmother's crepe recipe) to new (haven't you heard that mashed peas are the new avocado toast? You have now!), you'll find lots to try here.

DELICA'S SUPERFOOD MUFFINS

MAKES 12 MUFFINS

1½ cups all-purpose or gluten-free flour + more for flouring the muffin tins

1 cup quick-cooking oats

1 tsp baking soda

1 tsp baking powder

¾ tsp cinnamon

½ tsp kosher salt

½ cup packed light brown sugar

¾ cup coconut oil, melted, + more for greasing the muffin tins

1 apple, grated on a box grater

3 extra-large eggs

1 cup almond milk or any nut milk

½ cup finely chopped dried apricots

½ cup finely chopped dried prunes

½ cup finely chopped raw walnuts

Here is a favorite recipe from my old café, Delica Kitchen. These are dense in good nutrients, healthy fats and fiber. I use coconut oil and almond milk to keep these dairy-free, and I use gluten-free flour because my husband is gluten-intolerant. I make a big batch of these and freeze them for a perfect breakfast on the go. They feel like a treat (they are) but in a way that also feels virtuous.

Preheat the oven to 350°F and grease and flour a 12-cup muffin tin.

In a large bowl, mix together the flour, oats, baking soda, baking powder, cinnamon, salt and brown sugar.

In another bowl, whisk together the coconut oil, grated apple, eggs and almond milk. Stir the wet ingredients into the flour mixture and mix until just combined. Add in the dried fruits and nuts and stir again to combine.

Evenly divide the batter among the muffin-tin wells and bake for 20–25 minutes, or until a cake tester inserted into the center of a muffin comes out clean.

FRIED EGGS WITH SEAWEED, SESAME OIL & KIMCHI

SERVES 1

2–3 small sheets nori

1 Tbsp unsalted butter

2 eggs

2 rice cakes

Kosher salt and black pepper, to taste

1 tsp toasted sesame oil

2 Tbsp kimchi

1 tsp black sesame seeds

I make this for breakfast when the kids are gone and I have the house to myself. Table for one, please! Here is a case of a few simple steps that make something ordinary truly *extra*. Eggs are the perfect baseline for experimentation, and they do well with strong flavor additions (in this case, kimchi and sesame oil). Don't cook with toasted sesame oil—just a drizzle at the end will do it.

Finely slice the nori into long, thin strips and set aside.

Heat a small nonstick frying pan over medium heat for about 1 minute. Add the butter followed by the eggs. Fry, sunny-side up, until cooked to your liking. Placing a lid over the pan for a minute can help set the whites.

Place the rice cakes on a plate and top with the eggs. Season lightly with salt and pepper (kimchi is very salty, so go easy). Drizzle with the sesame oil and scatter around the kimchi, followed by the nori and sesame seeds. Enjoy immediately.

OATMEAL-STUFFED APPLES WITH MAPLE, WALNUTS & GREEK YOGURT

SERVES 4

½ tsp kosher salt

1¼ cups quick-cooking oats

2 Tbsp brown sugar

1 tsp cinnamon, divided

3 Tbsp unsalted butter

4 large Pink Lady or Gala apples

Juice of 1 lemon

½ cup plain Greek yogurt

¼ cup maple syrup

½ cup crushed, toasted walnuts

This is a bit of a show-off breakfast. Oatmeal . . . in an apple? What kind of sorcery is this? If you've never had baked oatmeal before, you're in for a real treat. This fuss-free baked breakfast dish is irresistibly rich and cozy. Like a warm hug in the morning, it's bound to make any day sweeter.

Preheat the oven to 400°F and line a baking sheet with parchment paper.

In a large pot, bring 2½ cups of water to a boil. Add the salt and stir in the oats, sugar and ½ teaspoon cinnamon. Once the oats are cooked, about 4–5 minutes, remove from the heat and stir in the butter until it melts.

Using a sharp knife, remove the top quarter (or "hat") of each apple. Using an ice-cream scoop, remove the core and some extra flesh inside the apples to create a cavity for the oatmeal. Be careful you don't scoop too deep and remove the bottom of the apples.

Place the apples on the lined baking sheet and squeeze lemon juice overtop. Sprinkle with the remaining ½ teaspoon cinnamon.

Spoon the oatmeal into the apples and bake for 20 minutes, until the apples are tender.

Remove from the oven and top each apple with a spoonful of Greek yogurt, followed by a drizzle of maple syrup and some toasted walnuts.

MAKE AHEAD
You can fully prep these the night before to save time and throw them into the oven in the morning.

BAKED EGGS, HARISSA RICE & ROASTED TOMATOES

**SERVES 2 GENEROUSLY
OR 4 SINGLE-EGG PORTIONS**

3 Tbsp olive oil

3 green onions, finely chopped

1 tsp grated garlic

2 Tbsp harissa paste

1 Tbsp tomato paste

2 cups cherry tomatoes, halved

3 cups cooked and cooled brown rice
(from 1 cup dry rice)

1 tsp kosher salt

Black pepper, to taste

4 eggs

1 Tbsp lemon juice

Flat-leaf parsley, for garnish

One of my favorite breakfasts is fried eggs on leftover rice with hot sauce. It's delicious for one, but tedious to make for a crowd. All those separate bowls, all that frying. This takes the frying, cleaning and dishes down to a bare minimum. To simplify the recipe (once you've gauged the hangover and/or the crowd), skip the onions, garlic and harissa and just top with a salsa or hot sauce after baking.

Preheat the oven to 375°F.

In a 9- or 10-inch cast-iron pan over medium-high heat, heat the olive oil for 1 minute. Add the green onions and garlic and sauté for another minute. Add the harissa and tomato paste and sauté for another minute. Add the tomatoes and toss until coated with the mixture. Stir in the cooked rice and coat well with the harissa mixture. Season with salt and pepper.

Using the back of a large spoon, pat down the top of the rice and create four divots in it. Crack an egg into each indentation. Place in the oven and bake for 10–12 minutes, until the egg whites are solid and the yolks are just set.

Finish with a squeeze of lemon juice, more salt and pepper and a handful of fresh parsley. Serve two eggs per person in bowls (or one egg per person if serving four).

MAKE AHEAD
Cook the rice up to 3 days ahead and keep it in the fridge.

MIXED BERRY BREAKFAST CRUMBLE WITH ALMONDS AND LIME

SERVES 6–8

2 cups blueberries

1 cup raspberries

1 cup blackberries

1 cup pitted cherries (use a mix of the other berries if you can't find these)

½ cup granulated sugar

Zest and juice of 1 lime

3 Tbsp all-purpose flour

TOPPING

1 cup all-purpose flour

1 tsp cinnamon

½ tsp kosher salt

¼ cup brown sugar

½ cup quick-cooking oats

½ cup slivered almonds

6 Tbsp (¾ stick) unsalted butter, room temperature

Plain Greek yogurt, for serving

Any dessert masked as breakfast gets a high score in our house. You can make this with any fruit; just follow the same proportions. I would do peaches in summer, frozen berries in winter, apples in the fall (okay—we are getting into dessert territory here). I love topping this with Greek yogurt—that tang is the perfect complement to the sweet fruit—which brings us back to breakfast territory again. The three tablespoons of flour in the berries thicken the juices so it's not too runny. You can also use cornstarch here for the same effect. I've subbed the all-purpose flour in the crumble for gluten-free before, and it works just as well.

Preheat the oven to 350°F.

If using frozen fruit, thaw in a sieve first, discarding any juice. Combine the blueberries, raspberries, blackberries, cherries, sugar, lime zest and juice, and flour in a large bowl. Toss together, making sure the berries are well coated. Transfer to a 9 × 13-inch baking dish.

For the topping, in a large bowl, mix together the flour, cinnamon, salt, brown sugar, oats, almonds and butter. Pinch and knead together with your fingers until the dough becomes soft and sticky. Keep pinching more than you think you need to. At first it will resemble coarse sand, but then it will begin to come together in stickier clumps, and by the end it should be quite moist and hold together when you pinch or squeeze it. Top the berries with an even layer of the crumble dough.

Bake for 50–60 minutes, until the crumble is cooked through, the juices are bubbling and the top is golden brown. Serve with Greek yogurt.

MAKE AHEAD

Make this the night before and pop it into the oven in the morning, but keep the filling and topping separate until the last minute. You could even make single-serve portions by baking them in ramekins.

SUPER NUT BUTTER

MAKES ABOUT 1¼ CUPS

1 cup raw almonds, skin on

½ cup raw walnuts

½ cup raw pecans

½ cup raw sunflower seeds

½ tsp cinnamon

1 tsp honey

¼ tsp kosher salt

We go through A LOT of almond butter in my house. About one jar per week. My eight-year-old has eaten it on toast with a little raspberry jam every morning for the last seven years. They say rituals are important. Needless to say, I've started experimenting with different nut butters to mix it up. Something with a little more complexity, sweetness, warmth. I spread this one on rice crackers with sliced bananas, apples or nectarines and a sprinkle of flaked salt. Don't be put off by the length of time this mixture needs in the blender (about 10 minutes); it's well worth it and prevents you from having to add any extra oil. Try playing around with different types of nuts—cashews, hazelnuts, Brazil nuts—maybe you'll land on something you love for a good seven-year stretch.

Preheat the oven to 350°F and line a baking sheet with parchment paper.

Scatter the almonds, walnuts and pecans on the baking sheet and roast for 10 minutes, until slightly toasted and fragrant. Allow to cool for 10 minutes.

Place the cooled nuts and the remaining ingredients in a high-speed blender. Blend on low for 1–2 minutes, periodically scraping down the sides of the blender. The mixture will first start to resemble an almond-meal texture—quite dry. Continue to blend on medium-low for another 8–10 minutes, scraping down the sides of the blender every minute or so. The mixture will slowly start releasing its oils and get creamier and creamier. Don't lose patience! Your blender will likely heat up quite a bit in the process, but just pause for 1 minute if it does. Once the texture is smooth, creamy and spreadable, remove it from the blender and place in an airtight container.

The super nut butter will keep in an airtight container at room temperature for up to 3 weeks.

NOTE

I love serving this on toast with sliced stone fruit on top.

MASHED PEA TOAST WITH A FRIED EGG

SERVES 4

2 cups frozen baby peas, thawed and warmed

½ cup plain Greek yogurt

2 Tbsp lemon juice

4 Tbsp olive oil, divided

¼ cup tightly packed mint leaves, roughly chopped

¼ cup tightly packed basil leaves, roughly chopped

½ tsp kosher salt + more for the eggs

Black pepper, to taste

4 slices toasted sourdough bread

4 extra-large eggs

1 tsp chili flakes, for garnish

This is one of those dishes that I will absolutely eat first thing in the morning but will just as happily have at lunch and at snack time. I love avocado toast (I'm a millennial—isn't that my birthright?), but it's time to create room for something else. Peas are high in protein, which makes this a great post-workout snack. (Did I lose you there?) And don't worry about having fresh peas; they are one of the only veg that I can say with confidence are just as good frozen as fresh. Avocados can't say that, can they?

In a high-speed blender (or with a hand blender), combine the peas, yogurt, lemon juice, 2 tablespoons of olive oil, mint, basil, ½ teaspoon salt and some pepper. Blend on low, until just incorporated. You will have to scrape down the sides of the blender once or twice. The mixture should still have some texture—you don't want a puree.

Spread the pea mixture evenly over the toasts.

In a large nonstick frying pan over high heat, heat the remaining 2 tablespoons of olive oil for 1 minute. Add the eggs and fry for 1 minute before flipping over and frying for 1 more minute. Finish with salt and pepper and chili flakes and place on top of the toasts. Serve immediately.

PAULETTE'S CREPES

SERVES 4

2 large eggs

1 cup all-purpose flour

1¾ cups whole milk

1 Tbsp granulated sugar

2 Tbsp melted unsalted butter
+ more for the pan

Pinch kosher salt

Fried eggs and bacon, for serving

My Belgian grandmother made these for me all the time, stuffed with cheese and sausages or simply sprinkled with lemon and sugar. They always felt a little more special than pancakes, and their versatility is to be admired. My kids will take a crepe with Nutella any day (because they are not fools; who wouldn't?). Crepes are faster to whip up than pancakes—no baking powder or soda here—and if you do up a big batch at once, you can keep them in the fridge and just warm them up in the morning. Hot crepe tip: the first one is always a bust, so just get used to throwing it out.

Preheat the oven to 200°F to keep the crepes warm.

In a medium bowl, whisk together the eggs, flour, milk, sugar, 2 tablespoons of melted butter and the salt. The batter should have the consistency of thick cream. Whisk in a touch more milk if necessary. Allow the batter to rest for 10 minutes.

In an 8-inch nonstick frying pan over high heat, heat a small knob of butter. Once the butter is melted and bubbling, pour about ⅓ cup of crepe batter into the center of the pan. Lift the pan up and swirl the batter around to coat the pan edge to edge.

Cook the crepe for 1 minute, then flip and cook for another minute. Slide out of the pan onto a plate and repeat with the remaining batter, adding a little more butter before each one. Keep the finished crepes warm in the oven until ready to serve.

You can top these with Nutella, lemon and sugar, breakfast sausages and Gruyère cheese, strawberries and whipped cream, or whatever you like. I, for one, put a fried egg and bacon in the middle and fold them into a little square.

OPEN-FACED SMOKED SALMON & AVOCADO OMELET

SERVES 4

3 Tbsp olive oil + more for drizzling

8 eggs, beaten

2 Tbsp finely chopped dill

2 Tbsp finely chopped chives

8 slices smoked salmon

8–10 cherry tomatoes, halved

½ avocado, sliced ¼ inch thick

2 handfuls arugula

½ tsp kosher salt

Black pepper, to taste

Juice of ½ lemon

This is the ultimate lazy omelet. Or a no-bake frittata, if you will. It can be sliced in wedges for a crowd and served right out of the pan, which makes it an ideal brunch dish. I would absolutely eat this for a quick lunch or dinner too. You can try this omelet with bacon, prosciutto or any cheese.

In an 8-inch nonstick skillet over medium-high heat, heat the olive oil. Whisk together the eggs, dill and chives. Pour into the heated pan and scramble with a wooden spoon or spatula for 10–15 seconds. Turn the heat to medium-low and, using a spatula, lift the outside edges of the egg up, tilting the pan so that the raw egg flows to the outside edge. Repeat the process until there is no liquid egg left in the center. It will still be a tiny bit wet, which is fine. Cover with a lid and cook on low heat for 1 minute to set the eggs.

Slide the omelet out onto a plate or serve it right from the pan, draping the smoked salmon pieces overtop, followed by the tomatoes, avocados and arugula. Season with the salt and pepper and finish with a good squeeze of lemon and a drizzle of olive oil.

SCRAMBLED EGGS 4 WAYS

SERVES 2

This will surely have purists rolling their eyes. I did a TikTok video with one of these methods and it got 1 million views, with comments ranging from "What sorcery is this?" to "Gordon Ramsay would riot" to simply "Nope." What can I say? They are controversial eggs. An Italian cook taught me the second version, which is sort of like a very sloppy and messed-up omelet. The internet may be outraged with my eggs, but I promise they all fall under the "don't knock it till you try it" category of cooking. Use a nonstick pan for all methods.

DINER-STYLE SCRAMBLED EGGS

4 eggs

¼ tsp kosher salt

Black pepper, to taste

1 Tbsp unsalted butter

Heat your pan over medium heat. Crack the eggs into a bowl and whisk well with the salt and pepper. Add the butter to the pan and swirl to coat the bottom. Add the eggs to the hot pan and immediately begin to stir with a spatula until about half-cooked. Turn the heat off and continue scrambling until the eggs are set. This will drastically help you in not overcooking the eggs.

ITALIAN RUNNY-YOLK SCRAMBLED EGGS

2 Tbsp olive oil

4 eggs

Kosher salt and black pepper, to taste

¼ tsp chili flakes

Heat your pan over high heat. Add the olive oil to the pan. Crack the eggs directly into the pan as if you were frying them. Let them set for about 30 seconds. Use a spatula very gently to start scrambling the egg whites, leaving the yolks intact. Once the egg whites are almost cooked, break the yolks with the spatula and stir them into the whites. The yolks should stay slightly runny and the result will be a ribbony yellow-and-white scramble. Season with salt, pepper and chili flakes.

FRENCH SCRAMBLED EGGS WITH CRÈME FRAÎCHE & CHIVES

4 eggs

¼ tsp kosher salt

Black pepper, to taste

2 Tbsp unsalted butter

2 Tbsp crème fraîche

1 tsp finely chopped chives

Heat your pan over medium-low heat. Crack the eggs into a bowl and whisk well with the salt and pepper. Melt the butter in the pan. Add the eggs and use a spatula to continuously scramble the eggs until half-cooked—this will take longer at a lower heat and result in a smaller curd. Add the crème fraîche and continue to scramble until the mixture is soft and glistening. Remove from the pan immediately and sprinkle with the chives.

AUSSIE FOLDED EGGS

4 eggs

¼ tsp kosher salt

Black pepper, to taste

1 Tbsp olive oil

1 Tbsp unsalted butter

½ avocado, sliced, for serving

Hot sauce, for serving

Heat your pan over medium heat. Crack the eggs into a bowl and whisk well with salt and pepper. Add 1 tablespoon of olive oil and 1 tablespoon of butter to the pan. Pour the eggs into the pan and allow them to set, without stirring, for 30 seconds. Using a spatula, very gently pull the sides of the eggs from the outer edges to the middle, allowing any raw egg to pour out onto the pan and cook. The eggs should look like a poorly made omelet. Remove when just cooked. Top with avocado slices and hot sauce.

Diner-Style Scrambled Eggs, recipe p. 120

Italian Runny-Yolk Scrambled Eggs, recipe p. 120

French Scrambled Eggs with Crème Fraîche & Chives, recipe p. 121

Aussie Folded Eggs, recipe p. 121

STRAWBERRY JAMMIES

MAKES 14–16

One 8 oz brick cream cheese, room temperature

½ cup unsalted butter, room temperature, + more for greasing

1 cup granulated sugar

2 large eggs

½ tsp almond extract

1¾ cups all-purpose flour + more for dusting

1 tsp baking powder

½ tsp baking soda

½ tsp kosher salt

¼ cup whole or 2% milk

About ½ cup strawberry jam

Powdered sugar, for dusting

These strawberry "jammies" were the most popular dessert at my beloved old café, Delica. We made them fresh every day for 10 years and would usually be sold out by mid-morning. Since closing, I often thought about making them, so I've adjusted the recipe for home use and they have now become a weekend staple in our house. They are rich, tender cakes that are spiked with a bit of almond extract and a sweet swirl of strawberry jam. I used to describe them to customers as somewhere between a scone and a donut. The cream cheese is the secret ingredient, giving them a slight tang and unbelievable flavor.

Preheat the oven to 350°F. Grease 12 muffin-top molds with butter and dust with flour.

In a bowl with a handheld mixer, or in the bowl of a stand mixer fitted with the paddle attachment, beat together the cream cheese, butter and sugar until light and fluffy, about 2 minutes. Scrape down the bowl, and add the eggs and almond extract and continue beating for another 2 minutes, or until pale yellow.

In a separate bowl, mix together the flour, baking powder, baking soda and salt. Add half of the flour mixture to the cream cheese mixture and beat until just combined. Scrape down the bowl and pour in the milk, followed by the remaining flour mixture, and mix until combined. Refrigerate the dough for 30 minutes.

Use an ice-cream scoop, if you have one, to divide the batter evenly between the muffin-top molds. Spoon about 1 teaspoon of strawberry jam on top of each jammy. Use the tip of a paring knife or toothpick to swirl the jam through the batter. The jam spreads when baking, so don't worry about getting this perfect. Refrigerate the batter in between baking and repeat the process with any leftover batter.

Bake for 22–25 minutes, until a cake tester inserted into the center of a jammy comes out clean. Cool for 15 minutes in the muffin tin before placing on a wire rack to cool completely. Dust with powdered sugar and serve.

NOTE
If you don't have a muffin-top tin, you can bake these in a regular muffin tin—you just might have to add a few more minutes to the baking time.

PASTA, GRAINS & FLATBREAD

I COULD WRITE A LOVE LETTER TO PASTA.

I would write it in swirly spaghetti letters and punctuate every line with a snappy cheese. I would thank it for being so comforting through my pregnancies, through travels and through tough family times. I would tell it I love it for its versatility, for its easygoing attitude and for feeding my family so fully.

But I'd be remiss not to mention my love of grains and flatbreads as well. Most (if not all) of the recipes in this chapter feature some kind of seasonal vegetable(s) and/or something to provide that fresh contrasting bite that pasta and grains love so dearly. There are comfort classics revisited, there are quick and easy meals, and there are sides here that I would pair with any number of proteins and happily eat for breakfast, lunch or dinner. (I told you, it's true love.)

I've also included a few of my favorite flatbread recipes that feature my next-best love: pizza dough. Secret's out, I don't make my own dough. I buy it, usually frozen from the grocery store. So sue me. When a shortcut this obvious is right in front of your eyes and yields great results, you can bet I'm taking it.

Let's make a bet that you have 95% (if not more) of the ingredients to make homemade gnocchi at home already. Go look. Right now. If I'm wrong, I'll send you a potato in the mail. If I'm right, we both win and you know what you're having for dinner tonight.

I remember making gnocchi with my son for the first time, and his reaction was so classic: "This is just like playdough, but we get to eat it!" How can anyone argue with that? It's fun to make, fuss-free and delicious. This recipe makes more gnocchi than you can likely eat, so throw any leftovers in a freezer bag for another day.

Here I have two variations for two very different outcomes. The first involves slightly more work on your end, but is oh so delicious. With deep fall/winter vibes, it's a crispy fried gnocchi worthy of a dinner party or a decadent weeknight meal. The second may be slightly more kid-friendly but is also a Gen X, millennial and Gen Y and Z pleaser too. The gnocchi get baked in the oven with your favorite tomato sauce and some mozzarella cheese for comfort-food perfection. Try one, try both, and reap the rewards.

HOMEMADE GNOCCHI 2 WAYS

MAKES ENOUGH GNOCCHI FOR BOTH RECIPES

GNOCCHI

4 baking or russet potatoes, peeled and boiled until tender

1 egg

1 tsp kosher salt

1½ cups all-purpose flour + more for dusting

Place the cooked potatoes in a large bowl and mash using a potato masher, ricer or box grater. It is imperative that the potatoes are very dry. Return them to the pot after mashing and stir for 2 minutes over medium-low heat to evaporate any remaining moisture. Transfer the potatoes back to the bowl, make a well in the center and add the egg, salt and flour.

Using a fork, begin to mix the egg and flour from the center of the well, working your way outwards to incorporate the potatoes.

Once you have a crumbly dough, switch to a large spoon and mix well to combine. If you find the dough sticky, add more flour. It should have the consistency of dry playdough.

Turn the dough out onto a floured work surface. Knead the dough several times and form it into a log shape. Cut 2-inch-thick strips off the log and roll each one into a long rope about 1 inch in diameter. Using a knife, cut the rope into 1-inch pieces and place on a flour-dusted baking sheet. Continue rolling and cutting the ropes until finished. You will have double what you need for a meal, so place any extra gnocchi in a flat layer in a ziplock bag and freeze. Cover the gnocchi with a clean, damp dishcloth while you roast the squash, if you're using that recipe.

BUTTERNUT SQUASH, SAGE & PECORINO GNOCCHI

SERVES 4–6

1 medium (about 2 lb) butternut squash, peeled, seeded and cut in 1-inch cubes

¼ cup olive oil

2 Tbsp balsamic vinegar

Kosher salt and black pepper, to taste

½ batch gnocchi (see opposite page)

½ cup unsalted butter

½ cup (about 30) sage leaves

1 tsp grated garlic

1 cup grated pecorino romano

Juice of ½ lemon

Preheat the oven to 425°F and line a baking sheet with parchment paper.

Place the squash cubes on the lined baking sheet and toss with the olive oil, balsamic vinegar, salt and pepper. Roast for 25–30 minutes, until tender and caramelized around the edges.

Meanwhile, bring a large pot of salted water to a boil on high. Cook the gnocchi in the boiling water for 3–4 minutes, or until the gnocchi float to the top of the water. Drain and set aside on a baking sheet or platter. Don't worry about keeping these warm as they will be fried before serving.

When the squash has finished roasting, heat your largest nonstick frying pan over medium-high heat. Melt the butter, then add the sage. Fry for 1 minute until the sage has slightly crisped up around the edges. Remove the sage leaves with a slotted spoon or tongs, and drain on paper towels, leaving as much melted butter in the pan as possible.

Add the gnocchi to the pan and toss to coat in the butter. The gnocchi should be in one layer, so you might have to do this in two batches depending on the size of your pan. Let the pieces fry without moving for 2–3 minutes per side, or until light brown and crisp. Add salt and pepper to taste.

Add the roasted squash and garlic to the pan and sauté with the gnocchi for 2 minutes.

Garnish with the fried sage, pecorino and squeeze of lemon juice and a little more salt and pepper.

BAKED TOMATO & CHEESE GNOCCHI

Olive oil, for greasing

½ batch gnocchi (see opposite page)

2 cups jarred tomato sauce

2 cups shredded mozzarella

Bring a large pot of salted water to a boil over high heat, and turn your oven broiler on high. Grease a casserole dish with the olive oil.

Lower the gnocchi into the boiling water and cook until the pieces have risen to the surface of the water, about 3–4 minutes. Remove with a slotted spoon, allowing all water to drain before placing them directly into the oiled casserole dish.

Spoon the tomato sauce over the gnocchi and lightly toss to coat. Top with the shredded cheese. If you are making this in advance, you can cover the dish with foil and refrigerate until ready to use. If you are eating it now, place the dish under the broiler for 3–4 minutes, keeping a close eye. The cheese should be bubbly and starting to brown. If baking later, preheat the oven to 425°F and bake (without foil) for 10–12 minutes. Broil at the end if needed.

(opposite) Butternut Squash, Sage & Pecorino Gnocchi, recipe p. 131

(above) Baked Tomato & Mozzarella Gnocchi, recipe p. 131

RIGATONI WITH ITALIAN SAUSAGE, RAPINI & PECORINO

SERVES 4

3 Tbsp olive oil

½ medium red onion, thinly sliced in half-moons

2 tsp grated garlic

1 tsp kosher salt + more to taste

Black pepper, to taste

4 mild Italian sausages, casings removed

1 tsp chili flakes (optional)

4–5 cups cremini mushrooms, cleaned and quartered

1 cup 35% cream

1 lb rigatoni

1 head rapini, washed and cut in 1-inch pieces, stems included

Zest and juice of 1 lemon

½ cup grated pecorino romano

This pasta is wintery, warming, a little spicy, creamy (not overly, just enough), toothy . . . just all around yum. Maybe leave the rapini out for the kids. Maybe not. Sub the cream with a little stock if you want to lighten it up a bit, but I'd suggest you leave it all in.

For the sauce, heat the olive oil in a large skillet over medium-high heat. Add the red onions, garlic, salt and pepper and sauté until fragrant and translucent, about 2 minutes.

Add the sausage meat and chili flakes and brown 5–6 minutes, using your spoon to break up the sausages into small pieces. Remove the sausage from the pan and set aside.

Add the mushrooms to the pan and sauté in the residual fat for 5 minutes. Pour in the cream and lower the heat to low. Allow the sauce to simmer for 3–4 minutes, until just thickened, then add the sausage back in. Turn off the heat and cover with a lid.

Cook the rigatoni in a large pot of salted boiling water for 8 minutes. Add the rapini to the pasta pot and cook for 1–2 minutes. Reserve 1 cup of pasta water and drain the pasta and rapini in a large colander.

Add the lemon zest, juice, drained pasta and rapini to the sauce and warm through. Add the pasta water, ¼ cup at a time, if needed to thin the sauce.

Season with more salt and pepper and top with grated pecorino.

ORZO WITH CHERRY TOMATOES, PANCETTA & BASIL

SERVES 6

2 cups orzo

3 Tbsp olive oil

1 cup cubed pancetta (¼-inch cubes)

1½ tsp grated garlic

1½ cups cherry tomatoes

1 tsp kosher salt

Black pepper, to taste

1 cup loosely packed basil leaves

Juice of ½ lemon

½ cup grated Parmigiano-Reggiano

When I was pregnant with my second son, I had terrible morning sickness. The only thing I wanted to (or could) eat was orzo with lots of Parm, butter and lemon zest. This food makes me feel better still. Now all my son wants to eat is pasta, even for breakfast. Considering how much pasta he consumed in the womb, scientists might argue that he's practically made of pasta, and you can't argue with science.

Bring a large pot of salted water to a boil over high heat. Cook the orzo for 8 minutes. Save ½ cup of the pasta water before draining the orzo in a colander.

In a large skillet over high heat, heat the olive oil. Add the cubed pancetta and cook until the fat has rendered and the pancetta is crispy, about 3–4 minutes.

Add the grated garlic and the tomatoes to the pan and sauté for 1–2 minutes, just until fragrant and the tomatoes are warm. Some tomatoes will burst and some will remain whole. Add the salt and some black pepper, followed by the ½ cup of pasta water.

Add the cooked orzo to the pan and warm through. Transfer to a large bowl and sprinkle with basil leaves, lemon juice and grated Parmigiano-Reggiano. Serve warm or at room temperature.

BAKED PASTA WITH MUSHROOMS & LEEKS

SERVES 4

4 Tbsp unsalted butter, divided,
+ more for buttering the dish

1½ lb assorted mushrooms
(cremini, button, shiitake, portobello),
sliced in ½-inch strips

1 tsp kosher salt, divided

¼ tsp black pepper

3 medium leeks, white and light green
parts only, sliced in ¼-inch rounds

3 cloves garlic, very thinly sliced

1 Tbsp thyme leaves

1 lb penne

8 oz Gruyère, cut in ½-inch cubes

½ cup grated Parmigiano-Reggiano

Gruyère is a favorite cheese of mine. It's Swiss cheese on steroids. Nutty and much more flavorful, but still entry-level for unadventurous eaters. In fact, as a tween, I used to put slices of Gruyère on a plate, microwave it and eat it with a fork. Edgy, right? This vegetarian baked pasta is simple enough for a weeknight dinner, but decadent enough for a dinner party. Be sure to undercook the pasta by about three minutes, as it will continue to cook in the oven. And don't season the mushrooms until they are cooked. The salt draws out water and prevents them from browning.

Preheat the oven to 375°F and bring a large pot of salted water to a boil over high heat. Grease a 3-quart baking dish with butter and set aside.

In a very large skillet over medium-high heat, melt 2 tablespoons of butter. Add the mushrooms and toss to coat in the butter. Leave the mushrooms in the pan without stirring for about 3–4 minutes, or until they begin to soften. Stir and allow to sear for a further 3–4 minutes, until all liquid has disappeared from the pan and the mushrooms are golden brown. Season with ½ teaspoon salt and the black pepper, and transfer to a bowl.

Return the pan to medium-high heat and add the remaining 2 tablespoons of butter. Add the leeks, garlic and remaining ½ teaspoon salt to the pan and sauté for 4–5 minutes, until the leeks are soft and wilted.

Add the mushrooms and thyme leaves to the pan and stir well to combine. Turn off the heat and set aside.

Add the pasta to the boiling water and cook for 7 minutes. The pasta will be very al dente. Reserve 1 cup of pasta water, then drain the pasta.

Add the pasta back to the empty pot along with ¾ cup pasta water and the leeks and mushrooms. Stir in the Gruyère.

Transfer the pasta to the greased baking dish, cover with foil and bake for 18–20 minutes. Remove from the oven and take off the foil. Stir the pasta, adding the remaining ¼ cup pasta water if dry. Sprinkle with the Parmigiano and bake, uncovered, for another 5 minutes. Serve warm.

10-MINUTE PASTA WITH ITALIAN TUNA, OLIVES & LEMON

SERVES 4

1 lb spaghetti

¼ cup olive oil + more for drizzling

2 tsp grated garlic

½ cup pitted green olives, roughly chopped

Two 5 oz cans Italian tuna in oil, drained

Zest and juice of 1 lemon

½ tsp kosher salt

Black pepper, to taste

3 cups loosely packed arugula

½ tsp chili flakes (optional)

You can literally make this dish in the time it takes to boil a pot of pasta, so it's impossible to say you don't have time to cook. As for the rest of the ingredients, I stopped buying canned tuna in water ages ago (unless I'm making a nice mayo-y tuna melt, in which case, only white flake tuna in water will do) and swapped out to Italian brands packed in olive oil like Callipo or Rio Mare, which can now be found virtually anywhere. I highly recommend you use a tinned tuna packed in oil for this recipe. Don't have olives? Use capers. Add some cherry tomatoes if you've got them.

Bring a large pot of salted water to a boil over high heat. Cook the spaghetti until al dente, about 8 minutes. Reserve ½ cup pasta water and drain the pasta.

In a frying pan over medium heat, heat the oil. Add the garlic and stir until fragrant, about 1 minute. Add the chopped olives, tuna, lemon zest and juice, salt, pepper and reserved pasta water. Toss with the pasta until warmed through. Remove from the heat and toss in the arugula. The residual heat will slightly wilt the arugula. Sprinkle with chili flakes and a final drizzle of olive oil.

SESAME SPINACH RICE

SERVES 4

1½ cups basmati rice

5 oz (1 small container) baby spinach

1 Tbsp toasted sesame oil

1 Tbsp soy sauce

½ tsp kosher salt

1 Tbsp white sesame seeds

Sriracha (optional)

I love this rice. I would eat it plain or accompanied by just about any meat or fish, so flag this one in your starchy sides stash—I promise you'll revisit it often. I feel almost silly calling this a recipe because it's so short and simple, but I think you might thank me for this at 6:14 p.m. on a Tuesday when you realize you still need to get dinner on the table for yourself and some hungry dictators. Please, please serve this with the Sweet & Sticky Glazed Meatballs on p. 203. They belong together. But if it's now 6:36 p.m. and you're desperate, top the rice with some fried eggs and hot sauce and call it a day.

Cook the basmati rice according to the package directions.

While the rice cooks, bring a large pot of water to a boil and prepare an ice bath. Once the water is boiling, plunge the spinach into the hot water for 1 minute, then immediately transfer to the ice bath. Once cool, use your hands to squeeze out any excess liquid. Transfer the spinach to a cutting board and roughly chop. In a large bowl, toss the spinach with the sesame oil, soy sauce, salt, sesame seeds and warm rice. Drizzle with sriracha for a little heat.

See photo p. 202

JEWELED RICE (APRICOT, TURMERIC & ALMOND RICE)

SERVES 4–6

1½ cups basmati rice

⅓ cup olive oil

1 cup dried apricots, sliced in ¼-inch strips

½ red onion, finely chopped

2 tsp grated garlic

1 tsp turmeric

½ tsp cumin

1 Tbsp orange zest

½ cup sliced almonds

1 tsp kosher salt

Black pepper, to taste

Juice of ½ lemon

We eat a lot of rice in our house. I almost always have a container of leftover jasmine or basmati rice sitting in the fridge waiting to go for fried rice, and you should do this too. Leftover rice is drier and doesn't clump. It gets crispy and never gets gloopy when mixing with other ingredients. Yes, this is just another fried rice recipe, but the combination of flavors may just surprise and delight you. Fragrant, sweet, salty, crunchy, earthy, golden. This is inspired by Iranian jeweled rice, with that beautiful deep-yellow hue and flecked with dried fruits and nuts. It's an absolute stunner next to the Miso Sesame Chicken on p. 180.

Cook the rice according to the package directions.

In a large frying pan over medium heat, heat the olive oil. Once hot, add the apricots, onions, garlic, turmeric and cumin. Sauté for 3–4 minutes, until the onions and garlic are translucent and lightly browned. Add the rice and toss to mix. Add the orange zest, almonds, salt and pepper. Finish with the lemon juice and serve.

QUINOA, PEAS & SUGAR SNAPS WITH CHARRED GREEN ONION VINAIGRETTE

SERVES 4–6

1½ cups quinoa

1 lemon

5 green onions, trimmed

2 Tbsp + ⅓ cup olive oil, divided

1½ tsp kosher salt

1 tsp chili flakes

1 cup fresh or frozen peas, thawed

1½ cups sugar snap peas, strings removed

½ cup loosely packed mint leaves

½ cup crumbled feta

This one is a fresh take. When I say "fresh," I'm referring to the snappy peas, herbs and lemony dressing, and when I say "take," I obviously mean take this to every backyard barbecue, work lunch and park picnic. The dressing is what really makes it pop. Charring the green onions will caramelize them and make a dressing that is tangy and sweet and herbaceous and unexpected. Be sure the quinoa is still warm when you toss it with the dressing as it will absorb better.

Cook the quinoa according to the package directions and keep warm.

Cut off one-third of the lemon, and slice it into 3 very thin rounds. Set aside. Using a vegetable peeler, peel 2 strips of zest from the remaining lemon. Julienne the zest and set aside. Reserve the peeled lemon for juicing.

Cut the green onions in thirds. Heat a medium-sized frying pan over high heat for 1 minute. Add 2 tablespoons of oil and swirl around the pan. Add the green onions and lemon rounds and allow them to deeply brown for 1 minute before flipping over. Continue cooking for another 1–2 minutes, until the onions are wilted and charred in some areas and the lemon rounds are brown and slightly caramelized. Place the onions and lemon rounds on a cutting board and finely chop.

Add the chopped green onions and lemon to a small bowl, followed by the juice from the remaining lemon, salt, chili flakes and remaining ⅓ cup of olive oil. Whisk together until combined. Pour over the warm cooked quinoa and toss well.

Add the peas and sugar snaps to the quinoa. Cover with a lid and allow the warm quinoa to slightly "cook" the vegetables for 5 minutes. You still want them crispy and bright green, so don't do this too far ahead of time.

Right before serving, roughly chop the mint leaves and scatter on top, along with the crumbled feta and julienned lemon peel. Toss loosely.

SOY BUTTER MUSHROOMS WITH BROWN RICE & HERBS

SERVES 4

1 cup brown basmati rice

2 Tbsp olive oil, divided

1 lb assorted mushrooms (cremini, button, shiitake), quartered

2 Tbsp butter

3 Tbsp soy sauce

2 cloves garlic

½ tsp kosher salt + more to taste

Black pepper, to taste

Juice of ½ lemon

2 Tbsp finely chopped chives

2 Tbsp finely chopped tarragon leaves (optional)

A beautiful buttery mix of mushrooms, sautéed until golden brown and spiked with umami soy. Sounds good, right? It is. This is a wholesome, wintery dish that I like to make with a steak or pork chops. If you're a fan of mushrooms (but even if you're not), you'll appreciate it. If there is one thing that Julia Child has taught me (there are a million things, actually), it is to not crowd your mushrooms in the pan. If there are too many in there, they get soggy and won't brown properly. Take the extra time and fry them in two batches. Also, never salt your mushrooms until after they are cooked (same goes for eggplant), as the salt releases water, another enemy of browning. I love serving this as a side with the Chicken Puttanesca-Style on p. 184.

Cook the rice according to package directions and keep warm.

In a large skillet over high heat, heat 1 tablespoon of the oil. When the oil is shimmering, add half of the mushrooms and stir to coat in the oil. Allow the mushrooms to sit in the pan without moving for about 2 minutes. Stir and allow them to sit again for another 2 minutes. Continue to sauté for another 4–5 minutes, until soft. Remove from the pan and repeat with the remaining 1 tablespoon of oil and mushrooms. Add the first batch of mushrooms back to the pan and add the butter, soy sauce and garlic. Sauté for 2 minutes to cook the garlic and slightly reduce the soy sauce.

In a large serving bowl, combine the rice, salt and black pepper. Toss the mushrooms with the warm rice. Taste for seasoning (it might need more salt) and add the lemon juice. Toss in the chives and tarragon leaves and serve.

NOTE
Another foolproof way to cook brown rice is in the oven. In a small, oven-safe dish, combine 1 cup of rice with 1¾ cups boiling water, 1 tablespoon butter and ½ teaspoon salt. Cover tightly with foil and bake at 375°F for 1 hour.

SAUSAGE RAGOUT WITH POLENTA

SERVES 6

¼ cup olive oil

1 large yellow onion, diced

1 Tbsp grated garlic

2 anchovy filets, roughly chopped

4 mild Italian sausages, casings removed

1 tsp kosher salt

Black pepper, to taste

½ cup dry white wine

One 28 oz can San Marzano tomatoes

Parmigiano-Reggiano, for serving

POLENTA

1 Tbsp kosher salt

2 cups polenta or coarse cornmeal (not instant)

¼ cup unsalted butter

A traditional ragout may simmer for at least a couple of hours. Delicious. This quick ragout will be done in about 30 minutes. Also delicious! Call me a cheater, but I'm taking the easy road here, which also comes down to my meat selection. Sausage is basically pre-seasoned ground meat with a generous fat content. We all know that fat equals flavor, so sausage is where it's at when we're looking to accelerate depth of flavor in a short amount of time. What do anchovies do? Oh, the exact same thing. It's pedal to the metal here, people. Start buying and freezing your sausages so you can whip this one up last-minute. My favorite way to serve it is scooped over a bowl of soft polenta, but you know it would also be delicious over pasta.

In a large saucepan or high-sided sauté pan with a tight-fitting lid, heat the oil over medium heat for 30 seconds. Add the onions and garlic. Cook for 6–7 minutes, until the onions are just starting to brown. Add the anchovies and stir to break down for 1–2 minutes.

Add the sausage meat, salt and pepper to the pan, using a spoon to break up the meat. Sauté until cooked through, about 5 minutes. Add the wine to the pan, scraping up any brown bits left on the bottom. When the wine has almost evaporated, add the tomatoes and their juices, crushing them by hand before adding them to the pan. Add ¼ cup of water, cover with the lid and simmer for 15 minutes.

While the sauce is simmering, cook the polenta by bringing 6 cups of water to a boil. Add the salt and slowly whisk in the polenta. Lower the heat to a simmer and whisk until thickened. Cover with a lid and cook for 25 minutes, stirring occasionally with a wooden spoon to prevent the polenta from burning on the bottom of the pan. Stir in the butter.

Spoon the polenta into a large serving bowl or individual bowls and top with the ragout. Finish with the Parmigiano-Reggiano.

MAKE AHEAD

The ragout can be made up to 3 days in advance and refrigerated.

Acorn Squash, Pecorino & Basil Flatbread, recipe p. 152

Nectarine, Prosciutto & Burrata Flatbread, recipe p. 153

Taleggio & Truffle Honey Flatbread, recipe p. 153

TRIO OF FLATBREAD

As you may or may not know, I come from a family of bakers. I grew up baking bread with my dad on the weekends from as early as I can remember. He was an avid *boulanger* who would experiment with natural starters and European methods that were completely unseen in North America in the 80s. He even built his own separate bake-house at our farm with a brick oven to perfect his craft. Fast-forward 10 years, and my parents' love for good bread continued to grow as they opened the first artisanal bakery in Toronto in 1992. ACE Bakery started small on King Street West, but grew to a size where it was shipping par-baked frozen baguettes and sourdoughs all over North America. You could even buy it in California! Pretty cool.

That background story is to inform you and the general population that although I'm an absolute lover of good bread, I don't make it myself. Are you shocked?! I'm a firm believer in outsourcing in that department. I'll bake a cake or tart or crumble any day of the week, but yeasted bread baking is not for me.

So here we are at these recipes for flatbread. Which, of course, include store-bought pizza dough. Where I'll take a pass on yeasted baking, I could write a love letter to frozen pizza dough. What can't it do? Bread knots, flatbread, cinnamon rolls, bread sticks, pizza pockets—the list goes on. I always have at least a couple of dough balls in the freezer. The best way to thaw your pizza dough is to put it on an oiled tray at room temperature and cover with plastic wrap for up to 4 hours before you want to cook with it (the owner of a pizza franchise told me this!).

Here are three varieties of flatbread/pizza/focaccia that work for a meal or for pre-dinner drinks.

ACORN SQUASH, PECORINO & BASIL FLATBREAD

SERVES 4–6

1 small, or ½ medium or large, acorn squash

6 Tbsp olive oil, divided

Kosher salt and black pepper, to taste

All-purpose flour, for dusting

One 25 oz ball store-bought pizza dough, thawed (see p. 151)

¼ cup good-quality homemade or store-bought basil pesto

¾ cup shaved pecorino romano

½ cup micro basil or torn basil leaves

1 Tbsp balsamic vinegar

Blind-baking is the simplest way to make flatbread, where we bake the dough on its own, with no toppings, until it is golden and crispy (about 10–15 minutes). I use this technique for all my pizzas and flatbreads and recommend you do the same. I like to call this one a "salad pizza," and I keep the squash seeds intact for more crunch (and less prep, obvs).

Preheat the oven to 450°F and line two large baking sheets with parchment paper.

Slice the acorn squash into ¼-inch rings, leaving the skin on and the seeds intact. Place the rounds on one of the lined baking sheets and drizzle with 2 tablespoons of olive oil and a sprinkle of salt and pepper. Bake for 20–25 minutes, or until the flesh and seeds are golden brown.

While the squash is baking, lightly flour your countertop and ball of dough. Use your hands to slightly flatten the dough, and then roll it out into an oval shape with a rolling pin or bottle of wine. The dough should be thin, but be careful to have it thick enough to support the toppings. Transfer to the second lined baking sheet, reshaping it if needed. Brush with 2 tablespoons of olive oil and sprinkle with salt. Prick the surface with a fork about 20 times. Blind-bake for 10–15 minutes, until golden and crispy.

Spread the pesto in an even layer over the cooked pizza dough, followed by the roasted squash with its seeds, pecorino, and basil. Drizzle the remaining 2 tablespoons of olive oil and balsamic vinegar overtop. Finish with a bit more salt and pepper.

MAKE AHEAD

If you like, you can cook the squash up to 3 days in advance and keep it in an airtight container in the fridge.

NECTARINE, PROSCIUTTO & BURRATA FLATBREAD

SERVES 4–6

One 25 oz ball store-bought pizza dough, thawed (see p. 151)

All-purpose flour, for dusting

3 Tbsp olive oil, divided

Kosher salt and black pepper, to taste

6 slices prosciutto

1–2 nectarines

½ ball burrata

1 large handful arugula

Juice of ½ lemon

This combo belongs with other epic pairings like peanut butter and jam, spaghetti and meatballs, and bacon and eggs. This could easily be a great salad if you didn't use the dough. But how fun is it for pizza night?

Preheat the oven to 450°F and line a baking sheet with parchment paper.

Lightly flour your countertop and ball of dough. Use your hands to slightly flatten the dough, and then roll it out into an oval shape with a rolling pin or bottle of wine. The dough should be thin, but be careful to have it thick enough to support the toppings. Transfer to the lined baking sheet, reshaping it if needed. Brush with 2 tablespoons of olive oil and sprinkle with salt. Prick the surface with a fork about 20 times. Blind-bake for 10–15 minutes, until golden and crispy.

Lay the prosciutto over the cooked pizza dough. Slice the nectarines into ¼-inch-thick wedges and scatter over the prosciutto.

Tear apart the burrata and evenly distribute overtop, followed by the arugula, salt and pepper, the lemon juice and the remaining 1 tablespoon of olive oil.

TALEGGIO & TRUFFLE HONEY FLATBREAD

SERVES 4–6

One 25 oz ball store-bought pizza dough, thawed (see p. 151)

All-purpose flour, for dusting

3 Tbsp olive oil, divided

Kosher salt, to taste

½ lb Taleggio cheese, sliced in ¼-inch slices

1 Tbsp finely chopped chives

1 Tbsp finely chopped rosemary leaves

Flaky sea salt and black pepper, to taste

2–3 Tbsp truffle or natural honey

Taleggio is a semisoft Italian cow's-milk cheese that is fairly mild and loves being melted. The shape of this flatbread mimics a giant calzone, but it will deflate after baking and return to its original form.

Preheat the oven to 450°F and line a baking sheet with parchment paper.

Lightly flour your countertop and ball of dough. Use your hands to slightly flatten the dough, and then roll it out into a large circle shape with a rolling pin or bottle of wine. Transfer to the lined baking sheet, reshaping it if needed. Brush with 2 tablespoons of olive oil and sprinkle with salt. Lay the cheese slices over one half the dough, leaving about a 1-inch border around the edge. Sprinkle with the fresh herbs. Fold the dough over the filling, and pinch well along the edge to seal the flatbread/calzone shut. Drizzle with the remaining 1 tablespoon of oil, and sprinkle with salt and pepper.

Bake for 15–20 minutes, until golden brown and puffed. Remove from the oven and cool for 10 minutes, during which time it will de-puff and go from a calzone back to a flatbread. Drizzle with truffle honey and cut into irregular triangles.

FISH

I LOVE FISH.

Dinner on the table in next to no time: fish. Versatility with your ingredients and flavors that pop: fish. Uncomplicated, family-friendly, fresh and breezy: fish, fish, fish. In case it's not clear, we eat a lot of fish throughout the week at home because it comes together so quickly and is so willing to adapt.

If you are able to buy your fish from a reputable fishmonger (as opposed to the grocery-store aisles), you should. From a health and sustainability standpoint, it's better for all. Exceptions include frozen shrimp, which seem to be decent from the freezer aisle. When you can, choose wild over farmed, and if farmed, choose organic. I know this seems like a lot of do's and don'ts, but if the only option is convenience (which I 100% understand), fish is still a healthy and versatile protein, especially if you're cutting back on your meat consumption.

Many of these recipes need minimal cleanup thanks to a single sheet pan or easy grilling, and a lot of them include sides and sauces that I would 100% throw on a piece of meat, or on eggs or rice, so feel free to pick them apart after you've tried them here. From a fresh riff on fish and chips with tartar sauce to individually wrapped parcels for dinner, we could have fish every night of the week and never tire of it.

BAKED HALIBUT WITH POTATO WEDGES & YOGURT TARTAR SAUCE

SERVES 4

2 large baking or russet potatoes, skin scrubbed well

6 Tbsp olive oil, divided

Kosher salt and black pepper, to taste

1 bunch broccolini

1 lemon, sliced in ¼-inch rounds

Four 6–8 oz pieces halibut

2 dill pickles, finely chopped

1 cup plain Greek yogurt

You know those days when cooking dinner seems like the last thing you want to do? YOU CAN DO THIS. It ticks all of the lazy cook's boxes. One pan, check. Virtually no dishes, please. Everything cooks at the same time, genius. Everyone's happy, it's healthy, it's easy and, best of all, it's good. See? All the boxes. Try it with salmon or cod, or truly any fish you like. The lazy cook's companion is pretty easygoing. I have a trick where I always roast my wedge fries balancing on their backs like poor little turtles that flipped over. This ensures maximum crispiness every time. (Plus, calling your potatoes turtles makes for good dinner-prep conversation.)

Preheat the oven to 400°F and line a large baking sheet with parchment paper.

Cut the potatoes into evenly sized wedges—roughly 12 wedges per potato. Place in a large bowl and toss with 2 tablespoons olive oil and some salt and pepper. Place skin side down (so they are balancing on their "backs") on one half of the lined baking sheet. This is important so the potatoes brown nicely on all sides. Bake for 15 minutes.

In the same bowl used for the potatoes, toss the broccolini with 2 tablespoons olive oil and some salt and pepper.

Remove the baking sheet with the potatoes from the oven and arrange the halibut down the middle of the pan, followed by the broccolini. Drizzle the fish with the remaining 2 tablespoons olive oil and some salt and pepper. Place one or two slices of lemon on top of each filet.

Bake the potatoes, fish and broccolini for 12–15 minutes, until the fish is firm and cooked through and the broccolini is tender.

Stir the dill pickles into the yogurt and serve with the fish.

SMOKED TROUT, BOILED POTATOES, JAMMY EGGS & WATERCRESS

SERVES 4

1½ lb baby yellow potatoes

4 large eggs

½ shallot, finely chopped

Juice of ½ lemon

1 Tbsp apple cider vinegar

1 tsp maple syrup

1 Tbsp Dijon mustard

Kosher salt and black pepper, to taste

¼ cup olive oil

4 cups loosely packed watercress

2 filets (about 1 lb) smoked trout, skin removed and broken into large pieces

This is a very nice lunch indeed. It's the sort of lunch that will make you feel like a real grown-up if you've been eating lots of rice cakes with random toppings from the back of your fridge (this is me!). This is a lunch that says, "I'm sophisticated, I'm traveled, I eat alone at restaurants with a glass of chilled grüner and the weekend *Financial Times*." This is also a mini lesson in how to make perfect jammy eggs—something that will take you far in life.

Bring a large pot of salted water to a boil over high heat. Boil the potatoes for 15–20 minutes, until tender but not falling apart. Drain, cool slightly and cut in half.

Place the eggs into a fresh pot of boiling water by slowly lowering them into the water with a spoon, ensuring they don't touch the side of the pot. (Cooking in boiling water instead of from cold ensures the shell will come off easily.) Cook for 7 minutes and prepare an ice bath. Once cooked, immediately transfer the eggs to the ice bath and leave for several minutes.

To make the dressing, whisk together the shallots, lemon juice, vinegar, maple syrup, Dijon, salt and pepper. Drizzle in the olive oil while whisking continuously.

Scatter the watercress on a large platter and toss with half the dressing.

Haphazardly place the smoked trout and potatoes over the watercress. Finish with a drizzle of the remaining dressing. Peel and cut the eggs in half and scatter them around the salad. If you want the eggs to look a little more rustic, split them in half with fork as opposed to cutting them. Finish with more salt and pepper.

MAKE AHEAD

Cook the eggs up to 3 days in advance and refrigerate. Bring to room temperature before serving.

SHEET-PAN SALMON WITH CHICKPEAS & BASIL-OLIVE SALSA

SERVES 4

¼ cup + 2 Tbsp olive oil, divided

1 Tbsp grated garlic

One 19 oz can chickpeas, drained and rinsed

2 cups grape tomatoes

1 tsp kosher salt, divided

Black pepper, to taste

Four 6–8 oz salmon filets

SALSA

1 cup tightly packed basil leaves

1 cup pitted green olives

1 tsp chili flakes

1 tsp grated garlic

Juice of 1 lemon

1 Tbsp red wine vinegar

¼ tsp kosher salt

Black pepper, to taste

¼ cup olive oil

Lemon wedges, for serving

I developed this dish for my Crumb cooking classes with the intention of building one-pan meals for my personal repertoire as well as for all the hungry, tired and working parents that I was teaching. It has proven to be a hit. (Am I allowed to toot my own horn here? *Toot toot!*) With only 5–10 minutes of prep, this dinner is on the table in 20 minutes from start to finish. It's one of my weekly go-tos that I make time and time again. The salsa is the secret that makes this dish special. If your children have sophisticated palates, they might really enjoy it. If not (like mine), just serve it on the side. It also goes well with grilled steak or chicken, so keep this salsa on hand as a fresh, easy topper for a protein any night of the week.

Preheat the oven to 375°F and line a large baking sheet with parchment paper.

On the baking sheet, toss together ¼ cup olive oil, garlic, chickpeas, tomatoes, ½ teaspoon salt and some pepper. Place the salmon filets on top, drizzle with the remaining 2 tablespoons of olive oil and sprinkle with the remaining ½ teaspoon salt and more pepper. Bake for 14–16 minutes depending on how pink you like your salmon.

To make the salsa, on a large cutting board, roughly chop the basil and olives together until they reach a salsa-like texture. Place in a mixing bowl and add the chili flakes, garlic, lemon juice, vinegar, salt, pepper and olive oil. Mix well to combine.

Remove the fish from the oven and top generously with the salsa. Serve straight from the baking sheet or transfer to a platter, with some lemon wedges for serving.

MAKE AHEAD

Assemble the fish up to the point of baking. Cover with plastic wrap and refrigerate. But make the salsa just before serving as the basil can turn color over time.

HERBY
SALMON SALAD

SERVES 4

A salad made mostly of herbs is a very good salad indeed. Add in some foolishly simple roasted salmon and a bright acidic vinaigrette, and you have more than a good salad—you have a near perfect one. The key here is making sure the salmon is at room temperature so it doesn't wilt said precious herbs. Obviously feel free to roast and cool the salmon the day before to make your life that much easier.

SALAD

1½ lb salmon filet

2 Tbsp olive oil

¾ tsp kosher salt

Black pepper, to taste

1 cup loosely packed flat-leaf parsley leaves

½ cup loosely packed dill fronds

1 cup loosely packed basil leaves

2 cups tightly packed arugula

2 Tbsp finely chopped chives

1½ cups grape or small cherry tomatoes, halved

VINAIGRETTE

½ tsp grated garlic

3 Tbsp lemon juice

1 Tbsp Dijon mustard

½ tsp kosher salt

½ tsp chili flakes

⅓ cup olive oil

Preheat the oven to 375°F and line a baking sheet with parchment paper.

Place the salmon on the lined baking sheet and rub with the olive oil, salt and pepper. Bake for 22–25 minutes, until cooked through and still a little rosy-pink in the middle. If using individual filets as opposed to one large filet, bake for 12–14 minutes. Allow to cool slightly while you make the vinaigrette.

In a small bowl, whisk together the garlic, lemon juice, mustard, salt and chili flakes until the salt dissolves. Slowly drizzle in the olive oil, whisking constantly.

In a large shallow serving bowl, toss together the parsley, dill, basil, arugula, chives and tomatoes with half the vinaigrette. Using your hands, remove the skin of the salmon and break the fish into large chunks. Scatter over the salad and drizzle over the remaining dressing.

MAKE AHEAD

Roast the salmon up to 2 days before and bring to room temperature before serving.

BUTTERFLIED GRILLED SHRIMP WITH CHARRED GREEN ONION YOGURT SAUCE

SERVES 4

24 (about 1½ lb) extra-large shrimp, tail on if possible

¼ cup + 1 Tbsp olive oil, divided

1 Tbsp grated garlic

Kosher salt and black pepper, to taste

6 green onions

1 cup plain Greek yogurt

Juice of ½ lemon

½ tsp cumin

Grilling fish on the barbecue can be tricky—lots of sticking, flaking and fish bits falling into the depths of the barbecue, never to be seen (or tasted!) again. Brutal. This dish couldn't be easier or faster, cooking in six minutes after a super-quick marinade of garlic oil, and you won't lose half of it in the process. Please seek out extra-large shrimp, as the recipe allots six shrimp per person. If you can't find extra-large shrimp, aim for a total weight of about one and a half pounds. You can serve this with lots of veggies and some rice or potatoes, or add some grilled flank steak for surf and turf. I love this with the Summer Ratatouille with Tahini Vinaigrette (p. 94) in the summer or the Slow-Roasted Baby Potatoes with Romesco Dipping Sauce (p. 86) in the colder months.

Heat your barbecue (or grill pan) to high.

Using kitchen shears, cut the shrimp down the back lengthwise from head to tail, leaving the tail intact so it is still connected in one piece. If using shrimp with no tail, repeat the same process, leaving ½ inch of flesh intact at the base.

In a medium-sized bowl, toss the shrimp with ¼ cup of oil, the grated garlic and a good pinch of salt and pepper. In another bowl, toss the green onions with the remaining 1 tablespoon of oil.

Place the shrimp and green onions on the barbecue. Grill for about 2–3 minutes per side. The shrimp will turn light pink and curl up when done, and the green onions should be bright green and charred in some places. Remove the shrimp and green onions from the heat.

Roughly chop the green onions and stir them into the Greek yogurt along with the lemon juice, cumin and some salt and pepper. Serve the shrimp on a platter with the sauce on the side.

MAKE AHEAD

You can pan-sear or grill the green onions on high heat beforehand. Let them cool before chopping and stirring into the yogurt. Store any extra yogurt sauce in the fridge for up to 3 days.

COCONUT SHRIMP WITH LIMEY FISH SAUCE

SERVES 4

1½ lb (about 24) extra-large shelled shrimp, deveined and tail on

1 cup all-purpose flour

3 eggs, beaten

1 cup panko

1 cup sweetened flaked coconut

1 tsp kosher salt + more for finishing

3 cups canola or safflower oil, for frying

¼ cup fish sauce

2 Tbsp maple syrup

Juice of 2 limes + wedges of 1 lime for serving

2 tsp sambal oelek or sriracha

The 90s called. And it said to eat all of the things that bring you joy. And these crunchy nuggets top the list! A bit of beach, a bit of sweetness, a lot of crunch. I make these whenever I want to pretend I'm on a tropical vacation (which is often, let's be honest). The citrusy fish sauce is the perfect accompaniment, as is the tequila on the rocks that you're about to pour.

Clean and pat the shrimp dry with paper towels. Place the flour in one bowl, the eggs in another and the panko and coconut together in a third. Add the salt to the panko-coconut mixture and combine.

Holding the tail, dip the shrimp one at a time into the flour, followed by the egg and finishing with the panko-coconut mixture. Press the panko-coconut mixture firmly onto the shrimp and set aside on a plate.

In a large high-sided skillet over high heat, heat the oil to between 365°F–375°F. Test the heat by adding a pinch of the panko mixture to the oil. It should begin to sizzle immediately. Place half of the shrimp in the pan and reduce the heat to medium. Cook for 1–2 minutes per side, until golden brown. Drain well on paper towels. Repeat with the remaining shrimp.

To make the sauce, whisk together the fish sauce, maple syrup, lime juice and sambal oelek. Serve alongside the shrimp with lime wedges.

CRISPY FRIED SQUID WITH OLD BAY AIOLI

SERVES 4

Don't be afraid to deep-fry every once in a while. Sure, it's intimidating, but it's easier than you think and the payoff is worth the effort. My whole family loves this dish, and as it is naturally gluten-free, my gluten-intolerant husband can get in on the fun. Squid is cheap as chips and neutral in flavor, which basically makes it a vehicle for crunchy deep-fried goodness and aioli. Dust off that can of Old Bay seasoning and put it front and center on the spice shelf because it's having a moment and that moment is now. Do make sure your squid is completely dry before dusting it in cornstarch, or it will be gloopy, and nobody likes a gloopy squid.

FRIED SQUID

3 cups canola or safflower oil, for frying

1 cup white rice flour

1 tsp Old Bay seasoning

½ tsp kosher salt + more to taste

1¼ cups cold pale beer or sparkling water

1¼ lb small squid, bodies cut in ¼-inch rings with kitchen shears (see note)

3 Tbsp cornstarch

Lemon wedges, for serving

OLD BAY AIOLI

⅔ cup mayonnaise

Juice of ½ lemon

2 tsp Old Bay seasoning

In a large, high-sided skillet over high heat, heat the oil to between 365°F and 375°F. Test the heat by adding a drop of the batter to the oil. It should begin to sizzle immediately.

In a medium bowl, whisk together the rice flour, Old Bay, salt and beer until smooth. Set aside.

For the aioli, in a small bowl, mix together the mayonnaise, lemon juice and Old Bay. Set aside.

Pat the squid completely dry with paper towels and place in a separate bowl. Add the cornstarch and toss well. Add the squid to the beer batter, one small handful at a time, and toss well to coat. Using a fork, pull the squid out one by one, allowing the excess batter to drip off before lowering into the oil. Keep in mind that the rice flour has a tendency to settle to the bottom of the bowl of batter, so whisk it every time you coat a new batch.

Cook the squid in the oil for 1–2 minutes, flipping over for another minute if they aren't completely submerged. The squid should be light golden and crispy. Using a slotted spoon or tongs, remove the squid from the oil and drain on paper towels. Sprinkle with salt. Serve hot with the aioli on the side and some lemon wedges.

NOTE
If you can't find fresh squid, a bag of frozen precut rings will work as well. Just follow the weight guidelines.

MAKE AHEAD
The aioli can be made up to 2 days in advance and refrigerated.

SNAPPER PARCELS WITH SESAME & SOY RICE NOODLES

SERVES 4

3 Tbsp maple syrup

¼ cup soy sauce

1 Tbsp toasted sesame oil

½ tsp kosher salt

Black pepper, to taste

Half 10 oz box pad thai rice noodles, cooked to package directions

Four 6–8 oz snapper filets, skin off (see note)

1 small handful cilantro

2 green onions, trimmed and finely sliced

Lime wedges, for serving

I just love writing a recipe that uses the word "parcel" so generously. Who doesn't love a parcel? I, for one, love a parcel. Especially when it's a parcel of food. You can even make these sweet parcels in the morning (in hardly any time at all) and bake them at the last minute (in hardly any more time). Every person gets a parcel, so there's no need to fight over portions come dinnertime. Serve each one with steamed bok choy, spinach or broccoli on the side and then go back and count how many times I used the word "parcel" on this one page alone.

Preheat the oven to 400°F.

In a small bowl, whisk together the maple syrup, soy sauce, sesame oil, salt and pepper.

Cut four parchment rectangles roughly 8 × 15 inches each. Divide the cooked noodles and place them in a pile in the center of each rectangle. Top with the fish, then evenly spoon the maple-soy sauce over each piece of fish. Scatter with cilantro and more salt and pepper.

Bundle up the parcel by joining the long edges of the parchment together and folding them to create a seal. Squeeze in the shorter sides and twist to seal, leaving space between the parchment and the fish so it can steam.

Place the parcels on a baking sheet and cook for 10–12 minutes, until the fish is cooked through.

Open the parcels and transfer the contents to four shallow serving bowls, or serve directly on the paper. Garnish with the green onions and a good squeeze of lime.

NOTE
A thin filet of white fish like branzino, pickerel or tilapia will also work well in this recipe.

MEAT

NO INTIMIDATING MEATS ALLOWED.

It should be on a lawn sign outside my front door.

When it comes to cooking meat, I am embracing every shortcut because I'm not going to sacrifice time or flavor. I believe we can have both (Don't we deserve both?).

In this chapter we are grilling (sometimes the same thing over and over because it is that good), we are eating outside and we are scraping up every last bit of sauce that has made these dishes special. We are slow-roasting and we are cooking everything in one pot, because enough with the dishes already! We are eating with our hands, we are stir-frying and we are self-saucing. There's something for everyone here: classics done in a new, more time-efficient way and creative hot takes inspired by a dill pickle chip.

Not intimidating, just yummy.

ONE-POT BAKED RISOTTO WITH CHICKEN

SERVES 4

4 chicken legs or 8 boneless, skin-on thighs

1½ tsp kosher salt, divided

Black pepper, to taste

1 Tbsp smoked paprika

2 Tbsp olive oil

1 medium yellow onion, diced

3 cloves garlic, finely chopped

2 Tbsp tomato paste

1½ cups arborio rice

½ cup dry white wine

4 cups chicken stock

½ butternut squash, peeled and cut in 1-inch cubes

3 cups packed baby spinach

Juice of ½ lemon

I promise you that risotto will be something you'll start making much more once you learn about this cooking process. Baking it, instead of constantly stirring, cooks it perfectly AND with zero risk of carpal tunnel syndrome. Everything—the chicken, the rice and the veggies—cooks in one pot, making this a weeknight-dinner dream dish. I like using dark meat (thighs and legs) as it's more forgiving when it comes to cooking time, and, let's face it, more flavorful.

Preheat the oven to 375°F.

Season the chicken on both sides with 1 teaspoon salt, pepper and smoked paprika. In a large heavy-bottomed, ovenproof pot with a lid, heat the olive oil over medium-high heat until almost smoking. Add the chicken skin side down. Allow to brown without moving for 5–6 minutes, or until the chicken comes away from the pan easily and is a medium golden brown. Flip the chicken over and cook for another 2 minutes. Remove from the pot with tongs and set aside on a large plate.

Adjust the heat to medium and sauté the onions and garlic in the chicken fat until translucent, 3–4 minutes. Add the tomato paste and cook for 1 more minute.

Add the rice to the pan and coat evenly with the mixture, cooking for 1 minute to toast the rice slightly. Deglaze with the wine, scraping up the caramelized bits from the bottom of the pan, until most of the liquid has been absorbed.

Add the chicken stock and season with the remaining ½ teaspoon salt and more pepper. Add the cubed squash to the pan along with the chicken, skin side up. Bring to a boil, cover with the lid and place in the oven for 30 minutes.

Remove the pot from the oven and scatter the spinach overtop. Place the lid back on and allow it to sit for 5 minutes to wilt. Uncover and season to taste with more salt, pepper and lemon juice.

MISO SESAME CHICKEN

SERVES 4

⅓ cup white miso paste

¼ cup honey

1 tsp grated garlic

4 chicken legs (you can use skin-on or skinless breasts if you prefer)

¼ cup white sesame seeds

Miso is a condiment that we all need. That salty, umami goodness brings so much to a dish by way of dressings and marinades, and we can't be mad at an ingredient that sits happily in the fridge for a good long time without spoiling. Here's a chicken dish that can come together in half an hour, no marinating required. I love serving this with Caramelized Cabbage with Peanuts, Green Onion & Soy Glaze on p. 73 or the Mashed Sweet Potatoes with Coconut Milk & Turmeric on p. 74.

Preheat the oven to 400°F and line a baking sheet with parchment paper.

In a large bowl, mix together the miso paste, honey and garlic. Add the chicken and toss well to coat.

Place the chicken on the lined baking sheet and spoon any remaining miso marinade overtop. Sprinkle evenly with sesame seeds.

Bake for 35 minutes, until the chicken is cooked through, the sesame seeds are nicely toasted and the miso glaze is starting to brown. If you are using chicken breasts, take 5 minutes off the cooking time. Drizzle any juices from the pan over the chicken.

MY FAVORITE DRUMSTICKS WITH PEANUTS & LIME

SERVES 4

12 chicken drumsticks

¼ cup soy sauce

¼ cup maple syrup

1 Tbsp grated garlic

1 Tbsp grated ginger

2 Tbsp corn, safflower or grapeseed oil
+ more for the chicken

¼ cup salted peanuts, roughly chopped

4–5 green onions, trimmed and
sliced in ¼-inch rounds

Lime wedges, for serving

Drumsticks are sort of impossible to screw up. Dark meat on a bone stays moist even if you overcook it. These are also excellent when done on the barbecue, so feel free to take this one outside. There was a while when I served these at every dinner party over the course of one summer. My husband, who, without fail, is lovingly supportive and grateful for everything I cook (minus the Whole Roasted Spiced Pineapple on p. 236, which he stands completely and utterly alone on), said sweetly to me, "Babe, I think you're starting to phone it in." My answer to that is that when I have guests over and they praise me profusely for something I make, I am sticking with it! So if you find yourself invited over to dinner (especially in the summer months of June to August), you're likely going to be eating these. Serve them with the Plum, Hazelnut, Frisée, Shallot & Parm Salad on p. 41 and the Quinoa, Peas & Sugar Snaps with Charred Green Onion Vinaigrette on p. 144.

Place the chicken drumsticks in a large freezer bag. Add the soy sauce, maple syrup, garlic, ginger and oil. Seal and shake well to coat. Ideally you can do this the night before, or a minimum of 1 hour before.

Preheat the oven to 425°F. Line a baking sheet with parchment paper.

Remove the chicken from the bag, shaking off any extra marinade, and place on the baking sheet. Pat the chicken dry with paper towels to remove excess moisture (the enemy of crispy skin). Drizzle with a little bit of oil and bake for 30–35 minutes, until the skin is crispy and dark brown.

Place the chicken on a large platter, and scatter with the chopped peanuts and green onions. Serve with lime wedges on the side.

CHICKEN PUTTANESCA-STYLE

SERVES 6

2 Tbsp olive oil

6 bone-in, skin-on chicken breast suprèmes
or legs, or a combo of both

1½ tsp kosher salt + more to taste

Black pepper, to taste

2 small yellow onions, diced

2 tsp grated garlic

6 anchovy filets, minced

One 28 oz can San Marzano tomatoes

½ cup dry white wine

¼ cup capers, rinsed

½ cup roughly chopped Kalamata olives

½ cup tightly packed basil, roughly chopped

Crusty bread or boiled potatoes, for serving

Briny capers, olives, salty anchovies and tangy tomatoes round out a classic puttanesca sauce. I brown the chicken and then smother it with that saucy goodness for a one-pot wonder that can be topped on potatoes or pasta or simply scooped up with crusty bread. This is an uncomplicated meal as welcome to my table on a Tuesday as is it on a Sunday night.

In a large Dutch oven or heavy-bottomed pot with a tight-fitting lid, heat the olive oil over high heat. Season the chicken on both sides with the salt and pepper. Add the chicken, skin side down, to the pot, searing for 5–6 minutes without moving, or until the skin is golden brown and crispy and releases easily from the pan. Flip and cook for 2 minutes on the other side. Transfer the chicken to a plate and set aside.

Turn the heat to medium and add the onions, garlic and salt and pepper. Sauté for 3–4 minutes until fragrant. Add the anchovies and stir for another minute. Add the tomatoes, crushing them first by hand, and their juices along with the wine, and bring to a simmer, scraping up any caramelized bits from the bottom of the pot. Place the chicken back in the pot, skin side up. Cover with a lid and simmer for 20–25 minutes, until the chicken is cooked through. Scatter the capers, olives and basil overtop and serve with crusty bread or boiled potatoes.

PICKLE-BRINED BIRD WITH ROASTED POTATOES

SERVES 4–6

4 lb whole chicken, left whole or cut into parts

2 cups dill pickle juice

¼ cup white vinegar

4 cloves garlic, roughly chopped

2 Tbsp kosher salt + more to taste

Black pepper, to taste

½ cup packed dill, roughly chopped + more for finishing

3 large Yukon Gold potatoes, unpeeled and cut in 2-inch chunks

Olive oil, for drizzling

A few dill pickles, sliced in spears, for serving

I warn you about this chicken. You will try this method and never be able to go back to any other type of roasted chicken again. I'm sorry in advance. Why am I apologizing? This is wonderful news. So sorry, not sorry. I created this recipe because I'm a dill pickle lover of sorts. A connoisseur. An addict, even. I buy dill pickle ornaments for my Christmas tree, I use dill pickle juice in my vinaigrettes, I make ice cubes of it for Bloody Marys. I've even put a dash in a martini. I love it (even if my puffy eyelids the next day don't). This chicken is figuratively drunk with pickle juice. As you go through your jars of pickles, save up any leftover juice, and if you start amassing enough of it, freeze it in storage bags. You'll start treating it like liquid gold. It's important to dry the chicken skin completely so it gets nice and crispy. My friend tested this recipe and exclaimed, "The skin is like a dill pickle chip!" This is what we're going for here. When the juices of the chicken drip down onto the potatoes, it's a venerable pickle frenzy. You're welcome.

The day before, find a deep bowl big enough to fit the bird plus the brining liquid. Make sure it's not metal, as the brine will react with it. If you are using cut parts of the bird (which is more than acceptable), use a large ziplock bag.

In the bowl or bag that will hold the chicken, mix together the pickle juice, vinegar, garlic, 1 cup water, 2 tablespoons of salt, pepper and dill until the salt has dissolved. Place the chicken in the brine and press down to submerge and fill the cavity, if using a whole chicken. It should be 75% submerged or more. Cover the bowl with plastic wrap (or close the ziplock bag) and refrigerate overnight.

When you are ready to cook the chicken, preheat the oven to 425°F.

Place the cut potatoes on a baking sheet, drizzle with some olive oil, sprinkle with salt and pepper and top with a wire rack. It is just fine if the potatoes are touching the wire. Remove the chicken from the brine, letting any excess brine drain from the bird, place it on the wire rack breast side up and pat dry very well with paper towels. Discard the brine.

Drizzle the chicken with olive oil and a good sprinkling of salt and pepper. Roast until the chicken is cooked through, about 55 minutes. If using cut pieces, adjust this time to 35–40 minutes. The chicken juices will drip down onto the potatoes and flavor them beautifully.

Carve the chicken and serve with the roasted potatoes and a few slices of pickles. Season the potatoes with salt and pepper to taste.

COCONUT TURMERIC GINGER CHICKEN

SERVES 4

One 14 fl oz can full-fat coconut milk, stirred well

1 tsp ground turmeric

2 tsp curry powder

1 Tbsp grated ginger

2 tsp grated garlic

1 Tbsp kosher salt

Black pepper, to taste

4 lb whole chicken, butterflied (see note)

1 Tbsp canola or safflower oil

One 10 oz package pad thai rice noodles

Cilantro leaves and lime wedges, for garnish

NOTE

To butterfly a whole chicken, place the chicken, breast side down, on a cutting board. Using kitchen shears, cut along both sides of the backbone, removing the spine completely. Turn the chicken over and point the wing tips towards the thighs. Use the palm of your hand to press down on the ribs of the chicken to flatten more.

Have you ever made a "self-saucing" chicken? You probably have, but haven't recognized it as such. We marinate the chicken, we keep the marinade, we cook the chicken, we turn the marinade into a sauce, we pour the sauce *allllll* over the finished chicken (and rice and noodles and anything else we can find because the sauce is just that good). A self-saucing chicken. Marinate the chicken in a large pot that you'll also put on the stove to reduce the sauce. Now you've self-sauced a chicken AND used only one dish. Aren't you clever. It's a classic pantry meal (all the seasonings used here are shelf-stable) and so deliciously coconut-y and fragrant. Serve it with my Whole Roasted Spiced Pineapple (p. 236) for dessert.

In a high-sided dish or bowl large enough to hold the butterflied chicken, whisk together the coconut milk, turmeric, curry powder, ginger, garlic, salt and pepper. I know this seems like a lot of salt, but this is seasoning a whole chicken plus the marinade that will be boiled down into a sauce.

Add the chicken to the dish with the marinade, breast side down, to submerge. Refrigerate in the marinade for a minimum of 2 hours and up to 1 day.

Preheat the oven to 425°F and line a baking sheet with parchment paper.

Remove the chicken from the fridge 30 minutes before cooking. The coconut milk might solidify in the fridge, but it will melt when you heat the sauce. Lift the chicken out of the marinade and wipe off as much marinade as possible back into the dish.

Place the chicken skin side up on the lined baking sheet. Transfer the marinade to a small or medium-sized saucepan and refrigerate. Rub the chicken skin with the oil. Roast the chicken for 45–55 minutes, or until the chicken is cooked through and the skin is a nice caramel color. To test for doneness, cut the skin between the leg and the breast. If the juices are clear, the chicken is cooked. If they are pink, return to the oven for another 5–10 minutes. Once cooked, allow the chicken to sit for 10 minutes while you make the sauce.

Place the saucepan of marinade over medium-high heat and bring to a low boil for 4–5 minutes to thicken the sauce and to ensure any raw chicken juices are cooked.

Cook the rice noodles according to package directions. Drain and place them in the bottom of a large shallow bowl. Quarter the chicken and place the pieces on top of the noodles. Spoon over the reduced sauce and garnish with cilantro and lime wedges.

LEG OF LAMB WITH HOT HONEY, FETA & OLIVES

SERVES 6 (WITH LEFTOVERS, MAYBE)

3 lb deboned or butterflied leg of lamb (ask your butcher to do this)

2 large Vidalia onions

1 Tbsp grated garlic

1½ Tbsp minced rosemary leaves

¼ cup olive oil

1 Tbsp + ½ tsp kosher salt, divided

1 tsp black pepper

¼ cup liquid honey

½ tsp chili flakes

1 Tbsp balsamic vinegar

½ cup crumbled feta

1 cup pitted green olives, roughly chopped

6 toasted pitas, halved

A leg of lamb can be . . . a lot. Some people don't like lamb for this, that and the other reason. Consider this your entry-level lamb dish (but fear not, you'll still come off as a pro). Start-to-finish time is about one hour, with most of that being hands off. The classic combo of feta and olives with lamb is bold and salty, and the hot honey just gives it the kiss of sweetness it needs for the flavors not to be too overwhelming. It's a fully composed meal if you serve it with pitas for making little handheld sandwiches. Or, if you prefer, the Cacio e Pepe Crispy Potato Cake on p. 85 and the Radish & Butter Lettuce Salad with Yogurt Dressing & Seeds on p. 45 would be great sides with this one. This is a meat that really requires a meat thermometer. I love mine; it's the answer to perfectly cooked meat, every time.

Preheat the oven to 375°F and allow the lamb to come to room temperature by taking it out of the fridge 30 minutes before cooking.

Cut the onions into ½-inch thick rounds and place in an even layer on a baking sheet.

In a small bowl, mix together the garlic, rosemary, olive oil, 1 tablespoon salt and the pepper to make a runny paste.

Some butchers or supermarkets will roll up the lamb in string—remove this and lay the lamb flat. If there are any thicker white fatty pieces, score them by cutting ¼-inch-deep slices into the fat, about ¼ inch apart. Place the lamb on top of the onions and rub the garlic-rosemary paste all over the lamb.

Roast the lamb for 40–50 minutes, or until the thickest part of the lamb registers 125°F for medium-rare.

Remove the lamb from the oven and allow it to sit for 15 minutes before slicing in ½-inch-thick pieces against the grain.

In a small saucepan over medium heat, combine the honey, chili flakes, balsamic vinegar, remaining ½ teaspoon salt and 2 table-spoons water. Stir with a fork as the honey melts. Bring to a frothy boil for 10 seconds, then remove from the heat and set aside. Rewarm slightly over low heat if you're not using this right away.

Arrange the roasted onions on a large platter and top with the sliced lamb. (I love piling the onions and lamb on top of some dandelion greens, but it's totally optional.) Scatter with the feta and olives, and finish with a drizzle of the hot honey. Serve with toasted pitas on the side.

THE ALL-IN-ONE BEEF STEW

SERVES 4–6

2 Tbsp olive oil, divided

5 slices thick-cut bacon, sliced in 1-inch pieces

2½ lb stewing beef, cut in 2-inch pieces

2 tsp kosher salt

½ tsp black pepper

1 large white onion, chopped in ¼-inch pieces

3 tsp grated garlic

2 large carrots, peeled and chopped in ½-inch pieces

2 stalks celery, chopped in ½-inch pieces

1 Tbsp smoked paprika

1 tsp cumin

1 tsp ground coriander

1 cup dry red wine or beer

One 28 oz can Roma tomatoes

3–4 cups chicken or beef stock

1½ lb baby potatoes, skin on

2 sprigs rosemary

Sour cream, for serving

Flat-leaf parsley, for serving

Sometimes you just feel like having a stew. A classic meat-and-potatoes stew that warms you from the inside out. Enter the all-in-one beef stew. And by all-in-one, I mean you've got your meat and potatoes all in one pot. I don't think it would be a bad idea to add a bright vinegary salad, but that's up to you. Start this on a lazy Sunday morning and enjoy it for a lazy Sunday dinner with crusty bread—and for leftovers the next day, because we all know what happens to those flavors when they get to hang out overnight. Don't let the ingredient list intimidate you. Most items in your pantry or fridge already.

Preheat the oven to 350°F.

Put 1 tablespoon of olive oil and the bacon in a cold large Dutch oven. Sauté over medium-high heat until the bacon is crisp. Remove the bacon with a slotted spoon and reserve the bacon fat in the pot.

Pat the beef dry with paper towels and season with the salt and pepper. Add the remaining 1 tablespoon of olive oil to the pot and add half the beef in one layer. Allow it to sear, undisturbed, for a few minutes on each side, about 10 minutes total, then transfer to a plate. Repeat this process with the second batch of beef, adding a little more oil if needed.

Remove the beef with tongs or a slotted spoon, leaving the residual fat and juices in the pan. Reduce the heat to medium and add the onions and garlic and sauté for 2–3 minutes. Add the carrots, celery, paprika, cumin and coriander and cook another 2 minutes.

Deglaze the pot with the wine and let it reduce by half. Add the tomatoes (crushing with your hands first) and 3 cups of stock and bring to a simmer. Return the beef and bacon to the pot and cover with a lid. Cook for 3 hours. Add another cup of stock if the liquid reduces too much.

After 3 hours, scatter the potatoes and rosemary over the stew—they do not need to be submerged in the liquid. Cover the pot with a lid and cook for 45 minutes.

Serve directly from the pot, with sour cream and a sprinkle of parsley.

SALT & PEPPER FLANK STEAK WITH QUICK TOMATO SHALLOT KIMCHI

SERVES 4–6

2 lb flank steak

2 Tbsp canola or safflower oil + extra

2½ tsp kosher salt, divided

½ tsp black pepper

1½ cups grape tomatoes

2 Tbsp distilled white vinegar

½ tsp grated garlic

2 tsp fish sauce

1 tsp honey

1 Tbsp toasted sesame oil

1 Tbsp sriracha

1 medium shallot, peeled and sliced as thinly as possible

1 cup loosely packed cilantro leaves and tender stems

1 Tbsp white sesame seeds

For weekly steak dinners, nothing serves me better than flank. It cooks in mere minutes and because it comes on the larger side, it's often big enough to serve the whole family. The tomato shallot kimchi is a condiment that I'm not sure how I did without in previous steak-eating occurrences. There is some strange alchemy that happens with the combination of ingredients that mimics a fermented flavor profile, but without having to put it in a jar under a rock for six weeks. Miracles do happen.

Remove the steak from the refrigerator 30 minutes before cooking. Rub with 2 tablespoons of vegetable oil, 2 teaspoons salt and the pepper, and set aside.

Cut the tomatoes in half and place into a bowl. Sprinkle the remaining ½ teaspoon salt over the tomatoes and toss. Let the tomatoes sit for 10–15 minutes to allow the juices to drain. Remove the tomatoes from the liquid and pat dry with paper towels. Discard the remaining liquid.

In another small bowl, whisk together the vinegar, garlic, fish sauce, honey, sesame oil and sriracha. Add the tomatoes and shallots to the bowl and toss to coat well. Let the tomatoes marinate while you cook the steak.

Heat a large skillet or grill pan over high heat for 2–3 minutes, until very hot. Using paper towels, blot any excess moisture off the steak. Rub a little more oil on both sides of the steak. Sear the steak for 5½ minutes per side for medium-rare, shifting the steak in the pan every 2 minutes. Set aside on a cutting board and let rest for a minimum of 10 minutes.

Slice the steak against the grain into ½-inch slices and lay out on a platter.

Toss the cilantro and sesame seeds with the tomatoes at the last second. Serve on the side or generously spoon over the steak.

PORK TONKATSU

SERVES 4

PORK

Four 8 oz boneless pork loins, 1 inch thick, trimmed of fat

⅔ cup all-purpose flour

2 eggs, beaten

3 cups panko

2 tsp kosher salt

1 cup safflower, canola or grapeseed oil, for frying, divided

4 Tbsp unsalted butter, divided

TONKATSU SAUCE

½ cup ketchup

3 Tbsp soy sauce

1 Tbsp red or white wine vinegar

1 tsp sambal oelek

I used to make chicken and veal scallopini all the time. Topped with an arugula and tomato salad, it's a perennial favorite. In fact, I ordered a big bone-in, dinner plate–sized veal scallopini prepared this way for my birthday several years in a row from one of my favorite restaurants. It's decadent and homey all at once. This dish hits the same notes, but with different flavor profiles. A more vinegary, more sweet/sour, more crunchy version, especially when served with the Fennel & Asian Pear Slaw on p. 50. Dare I say . . . more delicious.

Using a large knife, slice the pork loins in half lengthwise, splitting them into two flat pieces (for eight pieces total). Place the loins on a cutting board between two pieces of plastic wrap or wax paper. Use the bottom of a small saucepan to smack the pork to flatten it, "stretching" it from the middle outwards. It will end up about ¼ inch thick.

Place the flour, eggs and panko in three separate shallow bowls. Lightly whisk the eggs with 1 teaspoon of water. Add the salt to the panko and mix well.

One by one, dip the pork into the flour and coat on both sides. Dust off any excess flour and dip into the egg wash to coat completely, followed by the panko. Press the panko firmly onto each side. Continue with the remaining pieces of pork. Refrigerate on a plate until ready to cook.

To make the tonkatsu sauce, in a medium-sized bowl, whisk all the ingredients together. Set aside at room temperature until ready to serve.

Place a large skillet over medium-high heat. Add ½ cup oil and 2 tablespoons of butter to the pan. Test the oil by dropping in a pinch of panko. It should begin to sizzle immediately. Once the oil is ready, place four pieces of pork in the pan. Fry for 3 minutes per side, until crispy and golden brown. Place on a plate lined with paper towels. Use a paper towel to wipe out any remaining breadcrumbs and oil from the pan. Return the pan to the heat and repeat with the remaining oil, butter and four cutlets.

Serve on a plate with a few spoonfuls of tonkatsu sauce on the side.

Fennel & Asian Pear Slaw, recipe p. 50

STIR-FRIED PORK WITH PINEAPPLE & GREEN ONION

SERVES 6

Two 1 lb pork tenderloins, sliced in ¼-inch pieces

1½ Tbsp toasted sesame oil

⅔ cup soy sauce

¼ cup mirin or white vinegar

4 cloves garlic, finely chopped

3 Tbsp granulated sugar

3 Tbsp safflower, canola or grapeseed oil, divided

10 green onions, dark green tops removed and chopped in ½-inch pieces

1 cup finely chopped fresh pineapple

Cooked rice or rice noodles, to serve

⅓ cup roughly chopped salted peanuts (optional, for serving)

⅓ cup roughly chopped cilantro

Pork tenderloin is such an underrated meat and I honestly don't know why. It's lean, flavorful and cooks in a flash—perfect for a speedy weeknight dinner like this one. The salty-sweet marinade thickens and caramelizes while the pork cooks, intensifying in flavor and lending a deep caramel hue. Slicing the meat thinly before cooking means this is ready very quickly. I love this served over simple steamed rice.

In a large bowl, mix together the sliced pork, sesame oil, soy sauce, mirin, garlic and sugar. Place in the fridge and marinate for a minimum of 30 minutes and up to 1 day in advance. Drain the pork from the marinade, reserving it for later.

Heat a large nonstick skillet or wok over high heat, and add 1 tablespoon of the vegetable oil. When just starting to smoke, add half of the pork to the pan and stir-fry for 3 minutes. Once cooked, remove the pork to a bowl. Repeat this process with another 1 tablespoon oil and the remaining pork. Once all the pork is cooked and in the bowl, reduce the heat to medium-low. Add the last tablespoon of oil to the pan, followed by the green onions and pineapple. Sauté for 3 minutes, until the green onions are wilted and tender. Remove from the pan and set aside with the pork. Add the reserved marinade and ¼ cup water to the pan and bring to a low boil, cooking for 4–5 minutes to ensure food safety. Add the pork and pineapple back to the pan and warm through. Spoon over rice or rice noodles and garnish with roughly chopped peanuts, if using, and cilantro.

TURKEY LARB WITH CRISPY RICE NOODLES

SERVES 4

1 cup vegetable oil, for frying

One-third 8 oz package rice vermicelli noodles

Kosher salt, to taste

2 Tbsp fish sauce

3 Tbsp lime juice + a few wedges for serving

1 Tbsp white wine vinegar

7 green onions, finely chopped and dark green parts removed

½ tsp grated garlic

½ tsp chili flakes (optional)

1 tsp granulated sugar

1½ lb ground turkey or chicken

1 cup loosely packed basil leaves, roughly torn

Bibb lettuce leaves, for serving

Hoisin sauce, for serving

Hot sauce, for serving

A large serving bowl of this Laotian and northern Thai dish bursts with bright flavors and funkiness. Is "funky" a word that scares you when it comes to dinner? Well, if you enjoy the salty-sweetness of most southeast Asian dishes, chances are funk is a reason why. Fish sauce has a way of boosting the flavor of savory foods in a way that no other ingredient can. It's deeply salty, heavy on earthiness and subtly sweet. The addition of lime, basil, and fried noodles just takes this up to a whole other level of taste and texture.

In a large skillet over high heat, heat the oil for 2–3 minutes. Break up the vermicelli into loose strands. Test the heat of the oil by putting the end of a noodle halfway in. If the noodle "blooms" and puffs up, the oil is ready.

In two batches, add the vermicelli and fry until puffed and crispy on both sides, about 20 seconds. Remove with a slotted spoon and drain on paper towels. Sprinkle with a little salt. Turn off the heat and allow the oil in the pan to cool slightly before discarding all but 1 tablespoon.

In a large bowl, stir together the fish sauce, lime juice, vinegar, green onions, garlic, chili flakes and sugar, until the sugar has dissolved.

Heat the pan to medium-high and add the turkey to the pan, breaking it up with your spoon as it cooks. Cook for 5–6 minutes.

Add the turkey to the bowl with the sauce and toss well to coat. Add the basil and the crispy noodles and toss to break up the noodles. Season with more salt.

Spoon the turkey into the lettuce cups and serve with a dollop of hoisin sauce and lime wedges. I like hot sauce, but some don't. I'll leave it up to you.

MAKE AHEAD

The crispy rice noodles can be made up to 1 week in advance and kept in an airtight freezer bag at room temperature.

SWEET & STICKY GLAZED MEATBALLS

SERVES 4

I remember my mom serving me meatballs with lingonberry sauce when I was growing up. She spent her childhood years in Sweden, and cooking meatballs is a rite of passage that she passed along to us kids. I loved that salty-sweet combo then and still do now. This recipe is a riff on those meatballs, but jumping to another country altogether with Korean flavors that shine—fish sauce, soy, ginger and garlic—and sweetness from an apricot jam. It maintains top status as one of our personal family favorites, and Mom, the meatball maven, approves as well. Serve this with the Sesame Spinach Rice on p. 142 and dinner is dusted.

MEATBALLS

2 lb ground turkey

½ cup finely chopped green onions, white and light green parts only

1 tsp grated garlic

1 Tbsp grated ginger

½ cup panko

2 Tbsp soy sauce

2 Tbsp ketchup

1 Tbsp fish sauce

1 tsp kosher salt

GLAZE

⅓ cup soy sauce

3 Tbsp white or red wine vinegar

3 Tbsp apricot or fig jam

¼ cup ketchup

Preheat the oven to 400°F and line a baking sheet with parchment paper.

In a large bowl, mix all the meatball ingredients together. Using slightly wet hands, form 1½-inch-diameter balls and place them on the lined baking sheet. There should be about 20 meatballs.

In a small bowl, whisk together the glaze ingredients until the jam has dissolved. Brush (or spoon) half the glaze over the meatballs and bake for 15 minutes. At the 7-minute mark, baste with the remaining glaze.

If serving with the Sesame Spinach Rice, place the rice into a large shallow bowl and top with the meatballs. Spoon any extra glaze from the pan overtop.

MAKE AHEAD
Completely assemble the meatballs up to 1 day in advance and refrigerate.

DESSERTS

THE TRUTH OF THE MATTER IS

that I actually get the most joy in the kitchen when I'm baking. I find it by far the most relaxing way to cook—being precise, knowing exactly what result I will get if I am accurate, and the undeniable reward at the end of it all. And if you tell me you don't find extreme joy out of creaming butter and sugar or icing a cake, then you might want to seek professional help.

I love baking so much that I ended up ditching a French course one summer in Lyon to take the train two days later up to Paris to enroll in a traditional French pastry class at Le Cordon Bleu. I was all alone in the city, and after class I would wander around, hunting down the best patisseries, buying a pastry from each bakery (usually three or four a day), bringing them back to my flat and cutting off one bite out of each before writing meticulous tasting notes and then gifting the rest to the building concierge.

You may be surprised, then, to not find any real pastry techniques in this chapter (and you might even find store-bought puff pastry in here too). The recipes in this book are about what I cook for my friends and family in REAL life. Ask a pastry chef what he makes at home for his or her family—I highly doubt a Paris-Brest or Gateau St. Honore is on the list. At home I want simply delicious, nostalgic and "friendly" desserts that are relatively quick to make and that satisfy on a deep level.

Whether it's a decadent chocolate cake frosted to the nines, or a not-too-sweet nibble to finish off a meal (Halva? Of course!), I've had so much fun developing these recipes and I hope you find some of that same joy when you make them for your family and your guests.

LEMONY WHIPPED SHORTBREAD

MAKES ABOUT 28 COOKIES

2 cups salted butter, room temperature

1 cup powdered sugar

2 Tbsp tightly packed lemon zest (about 2½ lemons)

1 tsp vanilla extract

½ cup cornstarch

3 cups all-purpose flour

The text messages I get the most around the holidays usually involve baking queries. Do I have a good brittle recipe? (I do, but that's for another book.) Where do I order my gingerbread house from? What's an alternative to plum pudding? And always, always, what is my go-to shortbread recipe? All this talk of holiday season aside, this cookie is a treat any time of the year. It's packed with fresh lemon zest and whipped to within an inch of its life, so it's tender and undeniably melt-in-your-mouth. Use a timer here for when you're beating the batter—five minutes can feel like a long time, but every second coaxes the butter, flour and sugar into a fluffy mass of cloud-like dough that is addictive beyond measure. Salted butter, as we know, can do wonders to cookies, so don't skip on that.

Preheat the oven to 350°F and line two baking sheets with parchment paper.

In the bowl of a stand mixer fitted with the whisk attachment, or in a bowl with a handheld mixer, beat the butter and sugar on medium-high speed for 2 minutes, until very pale and fluffy. Turn off the mixer, then add the lemon zest, vanilla, cornstarch and flour. Start the mixer on low speed and slowly increase to high, beating for 5 minutes, until the batter is very fluffy and frosting-like in texture.

Using a 3-tablespoon ice-cream scoop with a handle release, scoop the batter, pressing along the side of the bowl to get a flat, even bottom. Release the dough and gently place the cookies 1 inch apart on the baking sheet. Do not flatten the dough. Bake for 15 minutes, until the edges just begin to brown.

Remove from the oven and allow to cool for 5 minutes before very carefully transferring the cookies to a wire rack to cool. Repeat the process with any remaining dough. The cookies will keep in an airtight container for up to 2 weeks.

MAKE AHEAD

You can make the batter up to 1 day in advance and keep it in the fridge.

BLUEBERRY & BLACKBERRY OAT CAKE

SERVES 10–12

1 cup quick-cooking oats, not instant

1 cup all-purpose flour

½ tsp baking powder

½ tsp baking soda

1 tsp kosher salt

1 cup unsalted butter, room temperature

1 cup brown sugar

2 large eggs

½ cup plain Greek yogurt

1 Tbsp vanilla extract

1½ Tbsp lemon zest

1 cup fresh blueberries

1 cup fresh blackberries

1 Tbsp demerara or granulated sugar

This cake could have ended up in the Weekend Adventures section as a loaf or a muffin (try it!). I love lemon zest with berries, and the hit of citrus is just the ticket for this mix of tart blackberries and sweet blueberries. Just a really lovely snacking cake. Serve it with Greek yogurt or crème fraîche.

Preheat the oven to 350°F.

In a medium bowl, stir together the oats, flour, baking powder, baking soda and salt.

In the bowl of a stand mixer fitted with the paddle attachment, or in a large bowl with a handheld mixer, cream the butter and sugar for 2 minutes. Add the eggs, yogurt, vanilla and zest and beat to combine for another minute.

Add the dry ingredients and beat for a further 10 seconds to combine. Use a spatula to hand-stir in the berries, being careful not to break them.

Spread the batter into a 9-inch springform pan. Sprinkle with the demerara sugar.

Bake for 40–45 minutes. The cake should be golden brown and slightly crisp on top, and a cake tester inserted into the center should come out clean. Allow to cool for 5 minutes before releasing the outer ring of the pan and cooling on a wire rack.

Serve slightly warm or at room temperature, and enjoy over the next 3 days.

This is one of those desserts that defies categorization. Is she a brownie? A pudding? Cake? How about all three? She likes to keep you guessing. What she lacks in identification, she makes up for in (quite sexy, might I admit) adjectives. She is molten and soft. She is warm. She is . . . spoonable (Is it getting hot in here?). A perfect and easygoing dessert for a crowd that leaves both adults and children endlessly comforted and happy. Everyone should know by now that chocolate and salt go together like a house on fire, so I've used salted butter here to give it that little edge of savory. Baking in a bain-marie (a water bath) at a low temperature keeps the pudding soft and jiggly, not cracked and overcooked. Serve with fresh berries and ice cream.

WARM BROWNIE PUDDING

SERVES 6

1 cup salted butter + more for greasing the dish

½ cup finely chopped bittersweet chocolate (70–80%)

¾ cup Dutch-process cocoa powder

½ cup all-purpose flour

2 Tbsp cornstarch

1 tsp baking powder

4 large eggs + 1 yolk

¾ cup granulated sugar

¾ cup brown sugar

1 tsp vanilla extract

Vanilla ice cream, for serving

Assorted berries, for serving

Preheat the oven to 325°F and butter a 2 quart oval or 9 × 9-inch square casserole dish.

In a saucepan over low heat, melt the butter and chocolate, stirring constantly until melted and glossy. Remove from the heat and set aside to cool slightly.

In a medium bowl, whisk together the cocoa powder, flour, cornstarch and baking powder.

In the bowl of a stand mixer fitted with the whisk attachment, or in a large bowl with a handheld mixer, beat the eggs, yolk and both sugars on high for 3 minutes until pale yellow and glossy. Add in the vanilla.

Add the cocoa-flour mixture in two batches, blending on low speed until just combined. Pour in the cooled butter-chocolate mixture and mix on low until blended.

Pour the batter into the casserole dish and place on a sheet pan or roasting pan with a 1- or 2-inch lip. Put the pan into the oven with the casserole dish inside it. Pour boiling water into the pan until it comes halfway up the side of the casserole dish. Be careful not to splash any water into the batter.

Bake for 40–45 minutes. The top will be firm and starting to crack around the outside, but the center should be slightly jiggly.

Allow to sit for 10 minutes before topping with vanilla ice cream and berries.

MAKE AHEAD
You can assemble the pudding up to the day before and keep it in the fridge until ready to bake.

CHOCOLATE CHIP CAKE COOKIES

MAKES 12 COOKIES

1 cup cold unsalted butter, cut in cubes

1 cup packed light brown sugar

½ cup granulated sugar

2 cold large eggs

1½ cups cake flour

½ cup all-purpose flour

1 tsp cornstarch

1 tsp baking soda

1 tsp kosher salt

3 cups 50% dark chocolate chips

Flaky sea salt, for finishing (optional)

This is a different kind of chocolate chip cookie, in that it uses cold ingredients, inspired by a technique used by Levain Bakery in New York. These cookies are ridiculously huge, so do take the time to measure out your ingredients just so and ensure your cooking time is consistent with the recipe. You don't want to improvise these ones. I use a scale to measure out each ball of cookie dough for the exact four and a half ounces. Some other tips for the perfect cake cookie? Cream the butter and sugar for the whole four minutes recommended—you don't want to feel any grains of sugar when you rub the butter and sugar between your fingers. Make sure your dough is cold before baking, and do not—no matter how tempting it may be—flatten the cookies. Go big or go home here! Baking them at a high temperature, along with the cold butter and eggs, ensures that the cookies don't spread too much and they stay almost cookie-dough-like in the center.

Preheat the oven to 410°F and line two baking sheets with parchment paper.

In the bowl of a stand mixer fitted with the paddle attachment, or in a large bowl with a handheld mixer, cream the butter and both sugars together for 4 minutes. It will start out very chunky and grainy, but will eventually become smooth.

Add the eggs one at a time, beating on high for about 10 seconds after each addition.

Scrape down the sides of the bowl and add the cake flour, all-purpose flour, cornstarch, baking soda and salt, mixing on low until just combined. Hand-stir in the chocolate chips.

Refrigerate the dough for a minimum of 1 hour.

Divide the dough into 4½-ounce balls and place on the lined baking sheets, 6 per sheet. Resist the urge to press them down. Bake for 12 minutes. The cookies will be nicely browned on the outside and still a bit doughy on the inside. Sprinkle with some flaky sea salt if that's your thing. It's definitely mine. The cookies store well in an airtight container for 2–3 days, but I doubt they'll make it that long.

SALTED CHOCOLATE & HAZELNUT SLAB CAKE

MAKES ONE DOUBLE-LAYER 12 × 18-INCH CAKE

CAKE

Unsalted butter, for greasing the pans

2½ cups all-purpose flour

1¼ cups Dutch-process cocoa powder

2½ tsp baking soda

1½ tsp baking powder

1 tsp kosher salt

2½ cups granulated sugar

3 large eggs

1¼ cups buttermilk

1¼ cups warm water

⅔ cup vegetable oil

FROSTING

1 cup unsalted butter, room temperature

½ cup Dutch-process cocoa powder

1 tsp vanilla extract

½ tsp kosher salt

5 cups powdered sugar, divided

½ cup whole or 2% milk, divided

TOPPING

1½ cups hazelnuts

1 tsp flaky sea salt, divided

Nothing gets my rocks off like frosting a cake with big swoops. This cake is that feeling. That pure-joy-of-baking feeling. The look and taste of unbridled baking joy. There's a certain nostalgia to it, in that it sort of resembles a grocery-store sheet cake. The method mimics a box cake too, where you dump all the wet ingredients into the dry ones and mix for three minutes. (The key to that nostalgic box cake lightness is in using oil instead of butter.) I bake this in two half sheet pans (12 × 18-inches) with straight sides. It bakes quickly because it is thin, so you can have more time getting your own rocks off decorating it.

Preheat the oven to 350°F.

Butter two half sheet pans. Place a trimmed sheet of parchment paper in the bottom of each pan and butter again.

For the cake, in a large bowl, add the flour, cocoa, baking soda, baking powder, salt and sugar, and whisk together.

In a separate bowl, place the eggs, buttermilk, warm water and the oil and beat with a handheld mixer on low speed until combined (feel free to use a stand mixer fitted with the whisk attachment if you prefer). Add the wet ingredients to the dry ingredients and mix on high for 3 minutes. Scrape down the sides of the bowl partway through mixing. Divide the cake mixture evenly between the pans.

Bake the cakes for about 22–25 minutes, or until a cake tester inserted into the center comes out clean. If your oven can be uneven, carefully rotate the cakes halfway through baking so they remain level. It is normal for the cakes to rise slightly in the center. Remove from the oven and cool in the pans on a wire rack for at least 15 minutes. Leave the oven on.

Place the hazelnuts on a baking sheet lined with parchment paper. Toast in the oven for 5–8 minutes, keeping a close eye. The skin on the hazelnuts will begin to crack and turn a very dark brown. Remove from the oven and place the nuts in the middle of a clean dishcloth. Gather the edges of the dishcloth and rub the hazelnuts vigorously to remove the skin. Discard the papery skins and place the hazelnuts on a cutting board. Carefully chop the hazelnuts (so they don't fly all over your kitchen) until they are finely chopped, then set aside.

To make the frosting, in a stand mixer fitted with the whisk attachment or using a handheld mixer, beat the butter and cocoa powder together until smooth. Add the vanilla, salt and half the powdered sugar and half the milk. Blend until combined, scrape down the sides of the bowl and beat again until light, fluffy and smooth, about 1 minute. Add the remaining sugar and milk and beat for 1 more minute. The frosting should be the color of milk chocolate.

Run a knife around the edge of the pans and very carefully flip the cakes onto a wire rack so they are upside down. Carefully peel off the paper.

When the cakes are completely cool to the touch, place one layer of the cake on a serving platter, keeping it upside down. Flipping the cakes upside down is an important step as this will make a cake that is flat as opposed to domed in the middle. Spread half of the frosting on the layer that's on the platter, making large swoops and leaving a ½-inch border around the sides of the cake. Scatter half of the hazelnuts and ½ teaspoon flaky sea salt across the icing.

Very carefully, using a spatula and your hands, place the top layer of cake over the bottom. Finish with the remaining frosting, hazelnuts and ½ teaspoon salt, using the same method as for the bottom layer.

The cake will keep covered in the fridge for 3 days.

MAKE AHEAD
Bake the cakes up to 1 day in advance, wrapping tightly in plastic wrap once cool. Store at room temperature. Make the frosting 1 day in advance and refrigerate in an airtight container. Allow both to come to room temperature before assembling.

See photo p. 207

UPSIDE-DOWN SKILLET APPLE CRUMBLE

SERVES 6–8

6 apples, such as Gala, Pink Lady or Golden Delicious

1 tsp cinnamon

1 tsp vanilla extract

2 Tbsp lemon juice

¼ cup unsalted butter + ¾ cup cold unsalted butter, cut in cubes, divided

⅔ cup packed light brown sugar

1 cup all-purpose flour

2 tsp baking powder

½ cup granulated sugar

½ tsp kosher salt

⅓ cup sour cream

When tarte tatin and apple crumble have a baby, you get this fall finery. Layers of apple, bubbling caramel and crispy crumble. Would it be cliché to call it a warm hug on a cool fall evening? A woolen sweater of sorts? A cozy fireside chat after a trip to the local fall fair? You get it. You'll need a cast-iron pan to pull this one off, so if you don't have one yet, let this be your gentle nudge, followed by a judgmental what-the-heck-are-you-doing-without-a-cast-iron-pan glare. You can serve this flipped onto a platter as the recipe suggests, or just spoon it right out of the pan. Cast-irons look so chic casually plunked in the middle of a table, so if you're not into the flip, you're still getting dessert points. (Just don't forget the vanilla ice cream.)

Preheat the oven to 375°F.

Core the unpeeled apples and slice each into eight wedges. In a bowl, toss with the cinnamon, vanilla and lemon juice.

In a 9-inch cast-iron skillet over medium heat, melt ¼ cup of butter, then add the brown sugar and 1 tablespoon of water. Stir to dissolve the sugar and cook until the mixture becomes smooth and dark and has a caramel-like consistency, about 1 minute.

Remove the pan from the heat and arrange the apples in an overlapping pattern around the outside of the pan working inwards (don't be too precious here about creating a perfect pattern). Create a second layer when necessary. Place the pan back on the heat and continue to cook on low while making the crumble.

In a medium-sized bowl, stir together the flour, baking powder, granulated sugar and salt. Add the ¾ cup cold cubed butter and, using your hands, pinch it together with the flour until the mixture resembles chunky, wet sand. Add the sour cream, using a fork to combine. Finish by using your hands to completely incorporate the sour cream. The mixture will become quite sticky.

Using your hands, drop the mixture over the apples, using a wet hand to press the dough down around the edges. You will not cover all of the apples and there will be some gaps in between. This is fine. It's meant to look rustic.

Bake for 45 minutes on a baking sheet (to avoid any caramel bubbling over), until golden brown and bubbling around the edges.

Remove the tart from the oven and immediately invert it onto a platter. As the apples cool, they are more likely to stick to the pan. If some apples stick, just place them on top of the tart with a fork.

CORNMEAL ALMOND CAKE WITH SUMMER STRAWBERRIES, YOGURT & BROWN SUGAR

SERVES 8

¾ cup unsalted butter, room temperature

⅔ cup granulated sugar

1 Tbsp vanilla extract

¾ cup fine cornmeal

2 cups fine almond flour

1½ tsp baking soda

1 tsp kosher salt

3 large eggs, beaten

1 cup plain Greek yogurt

10 strawberries, stems removed and cut in quarters

2 Tbsp light brown sugar

Call it a teacher's pet, but out of all the desserts in this chapter, I make this one the most. In the spring I use rhubarb, and in the winter I serve it with a grapefruit glaze. I've made it with blueberries, peaches, rosemary, standing on one foot and in the middle of the night. You get the idea. It's endlessly versatile and manages to get even better the day after it's baked, but will keep well for a solid four to five days. My husband eats very limited gluten, so he loves this one. The satisfying crunch from the cornmeal and the richness from the ground almonds lend an excellent texture play and a perfect base for whatever topping you're going with—in this case tangy yogurt and sweet summer strawberry. I made the mistake once of making my own almond flour by grinding raw almonds in a food processor. The results were disastrous. The cake ended up grainy and oily. Buy a fine almond meal or flour and you'll be guaranteed a foolproof cake.

Preheat the oven to 350°F. Line the bottom of a 9-inch spring-form pan with parchment paper. There is no need to grease or flour the pan.

In the bowl of a stand mixer fitted with the paddle attachment, or in a large bowl with a handheld mixer, cream the butter, sugar and vanilla until light and fluffy, 3–4 minutes.

In a medium-sized bowl, mix the cornmeal, almond flour, baking soda and salt together. Add the dry ingredients to the wet ingredients in thirds, alternating with the eggs, and mixing on low. Scrape down the bowl in between each addition and finish by mixing on high for 10 seconds. The finished batter is quite thick.

Spread the batter into the lined pan and smooth out the top.

Bake for 45–50 minutes, until the cake is golden brown and a cake tester inserted into the center comes out clean. Cool on a wire rack to room temperature or just slightly warm.

While the cake is cooling, line a sieve with a clean dishcloth. Place the yogurt into the sieve and place over a bowl for a minimum of 20 minutes. The goal is to remove any extra moisture from the yogurt which could make the cake soggy. Use a spatula to scrape the drained yogurt off the cloth and into a bowl. Spread the yogurt overtop of the cake, leaving a 1-inch border. Scatter with the strawberries and brown sugar. The brown sugar will start to melt into the yogurt, which is what we're looking for.

Another serving alternative is to serve the yogurt, berries and brown sugar on the side. The cake will keep longer ungarnished—if you're aiming for leftovers.

CLEMENTINE YOGURT PISTACHIO CAKE

MAKES ONE 5 × 9-INCH LOAF OR 12 CUPCAKES

CAKE

1⅓ cups all-purpose flour

½ cup fine almond flour

2 tsp baking powder

1 tsp kosher salt

½ cup chopped unsalted pistachios

1 cup vanilla Greek yogurt

½ cup granulated sugar

⅓ cup light brown sugar

3 large eggs

3 Tbsp packed clementine or orange zest

½ cup olive oil + more for greasing

GLAZE

1 cup powdered sugar

2 Tbsp clementine juice

3 Tbsp chopped unsalted pistachios

¼ tsp flaky sea salt

I call this my Chameleon Cake, because it can take on so many different flavors: lemon and almond, blood orange and pine nut, coconut and lime—just sub the flavors with the same measurements and you're good to go. Keep it rustic as a loaf cake or dress up your own chameleon with edible flowers in cupcake form. You won't even recognize it. I use sweetened vanilla Greek yogurt here, which, to be honest, I bought by accident. It turned out to be a happy one, as it allowed me to cut back on the granulated sugar.

Preheat the oven to 350°F and grease a 5 × 9-inch loaf pan with olive oil.

To make the cake, in a bowl, stir together the flour, almond flour, baking powder, salt and pistachios.

In another bowl, whisk together the yogurt, both sugars, eggs, zest and ½ cup olive oil.

Pour the wet ingredients into the dry ingredients and stir together using a wooden spoon or spatula until just combined. Don't overmix.

Pour the batter into the pan and bake for 40–50 minutes, or until a cake tester inserted into the center comes out clean.

Allow the cake to cool for 5 minutes before using a knife to loosen it from the sides of the pan. Remove to a wire rack.

To make the glaze, in a bowl, stir together the powdered sugar and clementine juice until smooth and glossy. It will be thicker than you think it should be, but it will spread once poured. Pour over the slightly cooled cake, letting it drip over the sides, and sprinkle with the chopped pistachios and flaky sea salt.

The cake will keep very well in an airtight container for 4–5 days.

FROZEN STRAWBERRY PAVLOVA WITH CHOCOLATE SHELL

SERVES 6

4 cups trimmed and quartered strawberries + a few more for garnish

½ cup granulated sugar

2 pints vanilla ice cream, softened at room temperature to stirrable consistency

3 cups roughly crushed store-bought meringues + extra for garnish

3½ oz dark chocolate (minimum 50%)

1 Tbsp coconut oil

Frozen pavlova sounds fancy-schmancy, but it really could not be more easy-peasy. This is entry-level desserting here. We're essentially reconstituting store-bought items, sticking them in a cake pan and freezing them. Doable, right? Super kid-friendly (both making and eating), and so breezy for entertaining—make it well ahead of time and just pull it out of the freezer before slicing and serving. If you like an Eton mess, if you like an ice-cream cake (if you don't, move along), you will love a frozen pavlova.

Place the strawberries and the sugar in a saucepan over medium heat, stirring constantly until the sugar is dissolved. Bring to a low boil for 3–4 minutes, until thickened. Spread out on a plate and place in the fridge to cool completely. It will be very liquidy but will thicken once cool.

In the bowl of a stand mixer fitted with the paddle attachment, or in a bowl with a handheld mixer, beat the ice cream on high for about 30 seconds, until softened. Mix in the meringues. Gently fold in the cold strawberries by hand, being careful not to mix them in completely.

Line the bottom of a 9-inch springform pan with parchment paper. Spoon the pavlova into the pan, smoothing the top. Cover with plastic wrap and freeze for a minimum of 2 hours, until set.

Before serving, melt the chocolate with the coconut oil in a small pan over low heat, stirring constantly until melted. Remove the pavlova from the freezer and peel off the plastic wrap. Release the sides of the cake pan and, using a pie lifter, remove the bottom part of the cake pan and parchment paper before placing the ice cream cake on a platter. Drizzle with the melted chocolate. The chocolate sauce will harden on contact with the frozen pavlova to become a shell.

Garnish with more berries and extra crushed meringues.

MAKE AHEAD
This can be made up to 1 week beforehand, without the chocolate shell and garnish, and kept in the freezer, wrapped tightly in plastic wrap and then foil.

BASQUE CHEESECAKE WITH BALSAMIC CHERRIES

SERVES 10

Four 8 oz bricks cream cheese, room temperature

1⅓ cups granulated sugar

Zest of 1 lemon

Zest of 1 lime

1 tsp vanilla extract

6 large eggs

2 cups 35% cream

⅓ cup all-purpose flour

TOPPING

1 cup pitted bing cherries (use frozen when not in season)

2 Tbsp balsamic vinegar (see note)

The first time I tried a Basque cheesecake was at Bar Raval in Toronto, where they have it out all day on the counter. It's lighter in texture than a New York cheesecake, a little less dense. A Basque cheesecake is now the only cheesecake I want to make because, as far as cheesecakes go, it's very forgiving. It doesn't require a water bath and you don't have to worry about cracking or burning the surface. In fact, you should actually try to burn the surface. How fun is that? Call me a rebel, but I'm also serving this one chilled. There, I said it, go ahead and clutch your pearls. It is SO rich (look at all that cream cheese!) that I find it's better with a bit of a chill, so I won't be leaving this one out on the counter all day. Eat it with a glass of sherry for extra culture points. How very Basque of you.

Place a rack in the bottom third of your oven, preheat the oven to 425°F and line a 9-inch springform pan with parchment paper. The parchment paper should stick up straight out of the sides of the pan, and you'll likely need two overlapping sheets. Don't fold it over, as it acts as a collar for the cake as it rises. Fold in the creases of the paper inside the pan so they lie somewhat flat against the sides of the pan. This should not be perfect—the wrinkles create a nice rippled effect on the outside of the cake.

In a stand mixer fitted with the paddle attachment, or in a large bowl with a handheld mixer, beat the cream cheese, sugar, both zests and vanilla for 1–2 minutes, until very smooth and glossy.

Add the eggs one by one, beating well after each addition. Add the cream and beat for another 15–30 seconds, until smooth and creamy. Sprinkle the flour over the batter and beat on low until combined and no lumps remain, about 20 seconds more.

Pour the batter into the lined pan, then place the pan on a baking sheet and bake for 55–60 minutes. The cake will puff up and turn a dark golden brown, almost the color of burnished chocolate.

Remove the cake and let cool in the pan on a wire rack for at least 3 hours before removing it from the pan and peeling back the parchment paper. If you have an hour to put it in the fridge, I advise it.

To make the topping, in a bowl, toss the cherries with the vinegar.

Transfer the cheesecake to a serving platter, slice and serve with the cherries. This cake will keep in the fridge for 2–3 days.

NOTE

The stickier the balsamic, the better. If you have a thin balsamic, boil ¼ cup of it with 1 teaspoon sugar for 3–4 minutes, until reduced and syrupy.

SALTED PEANUT & DARK CHOCOLATE HALVA

MAKES ONE 5 × 9-INCH SLAB, 2 INCHES THICK

1½ cups tahini

1 cup salted peanuts, roughly chopped, divided

1¼ cups granulated sugar

4 oz bittersweet chocolate (70%)

½ tsp flaky sea salt

This dessert is perfect for non-dessert people who just want a nibble. Put it out at the end of a meal with some Amaro and chilled fruit and feel like an actual entertaining doyen. The effortlessness! It also makes for an excellent host's gift, as it lasts for three weeks—just long enough to start that Halva SuperFan Club.

Line a 5 × 9-inch loaf pan with parchment paper, making sure the parchment hangs over the edges by a couple of inches. This will help you remove the halva once it is set.

Place the tahini in a medium-sized heatproof bowl (metal or glass) and mix in ½ cup of peanuts. In a small saucepan, combine the sugar and ¼ cup of water and place over medium heat. Stir until the sugar dissolves and then leave to come to a boil for 4–5 minutes, until a candy thermometer registers 250°F.

Very quickly, pour the hot sugar syrup over the tahini and mix vigorously with a spatula until the mixture comes together and pulls away from the outside of the bowl. If you mix slightly too long, your halva will turn out crumbly. The texture at this point should resemble stiff peanut butter.

Pour the halva into the lined loaf pan and smooth the top. Allow to cool at room temperature for 3–4 hours before removing from the pan.

Once cool, remove the parchment paper and place the halva on a wire rack. In a small pot, melt the chocolate over low heat, stirring until smooth and glossy. Pour the chocolate down the length of the halva and spread it in an even layer along the top and sides with an offset spatula or the back of a spoon.

Sprinkle with the remaining ½ cup chopped peanuts and flaky sea salt, and allow to cool completely, about 2–3 hours.

Slice thinly or cut in cubes to serve. The halva will keep in an airtight container for up to 3 weeks.

HONEY & PISTACHIO NECTARINE TART

SERVES 4–6

2 Tbsp flour, for dusting

One 7 oz square puff pastry, thawed if frozen

1½ Tbsp cornstarch

3–4 firm but ripe nectarines, sliced ½ inch thick

1 egg, beaten

1–2 Tbsp demerara sugar

1–2 Tbsp liquid honey

¼ cup salted pistachios, roughly chopped

Vanilla ice cream, for serving

This tart is perhaps the easiest dessert to pull off in the whole chapter. Frozen puff pastry gets rolled out and topped with peak summer nectarines. No pastes, no fillings, no creams. Then it's drizzled with honey and scattered with salted pistachios for a fun little nod to baklava. Bake this almost to the point of lightly burnt. I talk a lot about burning pies intentionally. It's a thing I wholeheartedly believe in. It's the secret to toasty, caramelized goodness, and though it feels counterintuitive, it's the key to crisp crust and deeply flavorful fruit. When I say "lightly burnt," I mean taking it about five minutes longer in the oven than you would normally consider. There should be some flecks of very dark caramelization and a couple of areas that look, in fact, a tad burnt. The bottom will be crisp instead of soft and the fruit will have an almost jammy gloss. Otherwise known as tart perfection.

Place a rack in the bottom third of your oven, preheat the oven to 400°F and line a baking sheet with parchment paper.

Lightly dust your countertop with flour and roll the pastry into a square that's ⅛ inch thick. Place onto the baking sheet. Dust the pastry with the cornstarch. This will absorb any extra juices from the nectarines as they cook.

Lay the nectarine slices on the pastry in rows, leaving about 1 inch of pastry around the edge. Brush the exposed edge of the pastry with the beaten egg and sprinkle with the demerara sugar.

Place the tart in the oven and bake for 30–35 minutes, or until the pastry is dark golden brown and the bottom is firm when you lift it with a spatula.

Remove the tart from the oven and place it directly on a wire rack so the air can circulate around it. When cooled slightly, drizzle with the honey and scatter with the pistachios. Serve with vanilla ice cream.

NO-CHURN VIETNAMESE COFFEE ICE CREAM

SERVES 6–8

Vietnamese coffee is strongly brewed dark-roast coffee topped with ice and a few tablespoons of sweetened condensed milk. It's rich, syrupy, icy cold and caffeinated. Otherwise known as a drink that has it all. I would actually consider serving it as dessert if it didn't send me into another orbit. But onto another subject entirely. Many people see an ice-cream recipe in a book and skip right over it. And for good reason—you need a machine that you probably don't have. This recipe takes the machine, tempering and fussiness right out of the equation. You pour your ice-cream mixture into a loaf pan and let it chill overnight. The next day you are rewarded with the creamiest, scoopable ice cream. Otherwise known as an ice cream that has it all.

1 oz shot warm espresso

¼ tsp cinnamon

2 Tbsp instant coffee granules

One 10 oz can sweetened condensed milk

2 cups whipping cream

In a large bowl, whisk together the warm espresso, cinnamon and instant coffee to dissolve. Add the condensed milk and whisk until well combined.

In a separate bowl, using a handheld mixer, whip the whipping cream to stiff peaks, about 3 minutes.

Add the condensed milk mixture to the whipped cream, using a spatula to gently fold it together. Pour into a 5 × 9-inch loaf tin and cover the surface directly with plastic wrap. Freeze for at least 24 hours and allow to soften at room temperature for 10 minutes before serving.

MAKE AHEAD

This can be made up to 5 days in advance. After that, the ice cream begins to crystalize slightly.

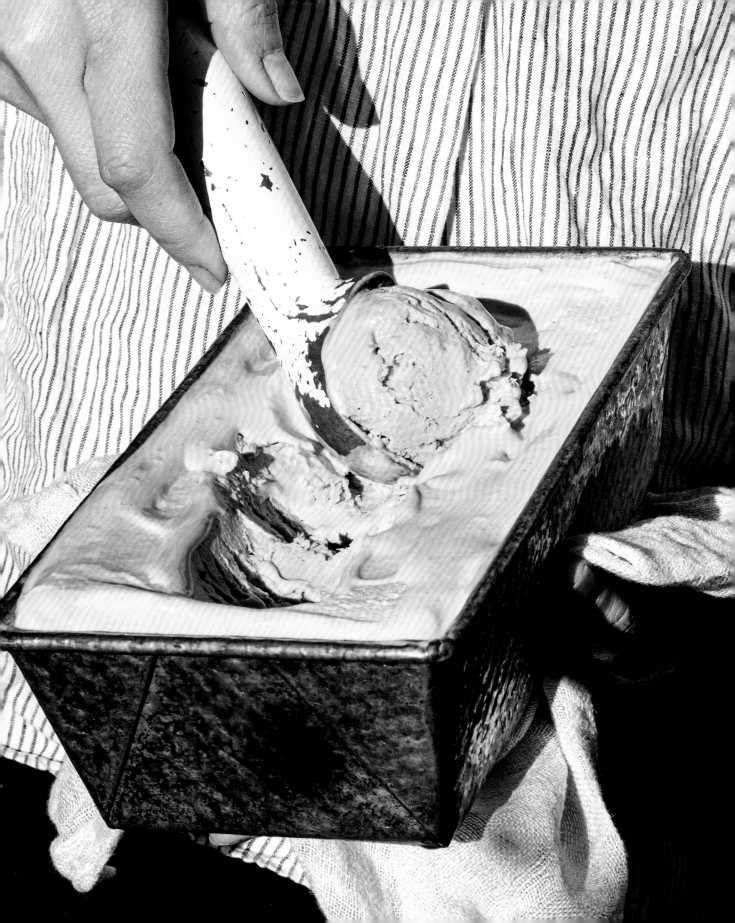

LEMON PUDDING WITH SALTED GRAHAM CRUMB

SERVES 6

4 cups whipping cream

1½ cups granulated sugar

3 Tbsp lemon zest

¾ cup lemon juice

½ cup graham cracker crumbs

½ tsp kosher salt

I think this dessert is a bit of a revelation. The pudding requires no tempering of eggs and has only three ingredients: cream, lemon and sugar. It's truly dead simple. It reminds me of the inside of a lemon meringue pie—mouth-puckeringly tart and sweet, except a little creamier. Topped with some salted graham cracker crumbs, it has crunch and silkiness. This must be made the day before, with the salted graham crumble sprinkled on right before serving.

In a heavy-bottomed pot over medium heat, boil the whipping cream, sugar and lemon zest for 8–10 minutes, or until reduced by about one-third.

Remove the pot from the heat and stir in the lemon juice. The mixture will begin to thicken slightly. Transfer the mixture to a large pitcher to avoid splashes. Pour the mixture into six glasses and chill, uncovered, for 2 hours, then cover with plastic wrap and chill overnight to set. The consistency should end up like smooth creamy yogurt.

Before serving, mix the graham cracker crumbs with the salt. Spoon 1½ tablespoons of crumbs over each lemon pudding.

WHOLE ROASTED SPICED PINEAPPLE

SERVES 6

1 whole pineapple

3 Tbsp brown sugar

1 tsp cinnamon

½ tsp ground ginger

Vanilla ice cream, for serving

This is a FUN dessert. It's sort of retro, sort of weird and majorly delicious. The presentation of the full pineapple with the leaves intact feels celebratory and it's just as comfortable capping off a fancy dinner party (with silver carving utensils and all) as it is at a backyard barbecue. The trick for selecting a ripe pineapple is to tug on the inner leaves. If they pull out easily, the pineapple is ripe. The simple dry spice rub of cinnamon, ginger and brown sugar works beautifully with the sweet and sour fruit, and I wouldn't be mad at all if you drizzled over a couple of tablespoons of dark rum after roasting, for that Caribbean vibe.

Preheat the oven to 400°F and line a baking sheet with parchment paper.

Peel the pineapple by cutting off the bottom ½ inch. Place the cut side on a cutting board and run the knife along the outside of the pineapple from the top to the bottom, removing the tough skin and making sure to remove any of the eyes and small brown seeds. Leave the top leaves of the pineapple intact.

In a small bowl, mix together the brown sugar, cinnamon and ginger. Place the cut pineapple on the lined baking sheet and rub with the spice mixture.

Bake for 1 hour, or until brown and sticky. Remove the pineapple from the oven and cut in 1½-inch slices. Serve with a scoop of vanilla ice cream.

ACKNOWLEDGMENTS

Writing and developing recipes has been one of the great joys of my life. I don't remember a time when the kitchen wasn't the center of my home life or professional life. This book feels like a great landmark in bringing my passion to tangible fruition. Like most good things in my life, this has been a massive group effort with the help of people I admire and trust implicitly.

Let me begin with my mother, Linda Haynes, who, whether she planned to or not, instilled a passion for cooking and the family table in me. It runs so deep that food and gathering with the ones I love is the paramount priority of my life. She encouraged me to do this book and acted as my chief recipe tester, sounding board and editor.

To my husband, Darcy, for always, ALWAYS saying everything tasted great even when I knew it didn't, and for being my sounding board on creative ideas and gladly cleaning up all the dishes.

To my boys, Marty and Wynn, who already show a keen interest at the stove. I hope this book is something you'll come back to for years to come and that it will remind you of these messy, crazy, joyous days. Sitting down at the table with you at the end of the day is always my rose.

To Dad, I hope I've made you proud. Your wisdom and unconditional love are something I rely on heavily. To Seanna, John and Lindsey, who have always been the kindest, most loving and generous siblings a little sister could hope for. To Luke, who shares my great love of cooking and eating. Some of my favorite times with you have been cooking together or just talking about great meals we've had. Thank you for taking the reins at Delica when I couldn't (or didn't want to). I know how hard you worked, and I want you to know that. I love you.

To Deirdre, Nate, Mookie and Julie. I can't believe I get to call you my family. Thank you for your encouragement over the years and for testing many, MANY of my recipes, good and bad.

To JJ and Saverina. I love you and will always remember sharing lots of wonderful meals with you whether on Lake Simcoe or in Siena.

To Courtney Wotherspoon, my best friend and forever creative collaborator. You helped me find a voice for this book when I couldn't. You've been a key part of this project, helping with everything from recipe testing, writing, editing and creative direction. What can't you do, my dear?

To Louisa Nicolaou and Justine Brady. Photographer and food stylist respectively. You both understood from the get-go exactly what I wanted to achieve and turned out images that are better than I could have ever imagined. Every day working with you was a dream come true.

To Maddy Slatt, for keeping the shoots running smoothly and for being such an amazing support with Crumb.

To Deb Belcourt, for providing me with endless support with Crumb and for promoting this book. I deeply appreciate your friendship and mentoring.

To Lynn Fernandez, who cleaned THE MOST DISHES, bought all the groceries and gave me excellent support and feedback on all the recipes.

To Zoe Maslow. The best editor this side of the Mississippi. Your steady encouragement and brilliant comments and critiques made this book infinitely better. You kept me on time and gave me the space I needed to do my thing. Thank you for everything! You're the unsung hero of the book world.

To Robert McCullough, the first person who really believed in this book and fulfilled my dreams. You were patient and encouraging and so supportive. Thank you for giving me a chance. I hope I've made you happy! And thank you to the Penguin Random House team for all of the support in bringing this to life.

To Kelly Hill, who right off the bat understood the look and feel of how I envisioned this book. Working with you felt so intuitive and easy. Thank you for giving life and color to these pages.

To my dear friends (you know who you are) who I've spent hours with over many meals bursting at the seams with laughter and getting up to no good. I'd be lost without you.

INDEX

DEVIN CONNELL

is the founder of the popular website This Is Crumb, as well as a cookbook author, recipe developer and Food Network Canada personality. She also founded Delica Kitchen, a catering company and small group of restaurants in Toronto. A wife and mother of two boys, she's no stranger to a messy kitchen.

@thisiscrumb
www.thisiscrumb.com

Cover design by Kelly Hill
Cover photography by Louisa Nicolaou

appetite
by RANDOM HOUSE

www.penguinrandomhouse.ca